# Participatory Literacy Education

Arlene Fingeret, *Editor*
*North Carolina State University*

Paul Jurmo, *Editor*
*Business Council for Effective Literacy*

**NEW DIRECTIONS FOR CONTINUING EDUCATION**

RALPH G. BROCKETT, *Editor-in-Chief*
*University of Tennessee, Knoxville*

ALAN B. KNOX, *Consulting Editor*
*University of Wisconsin*

Number 42, Summer 1989

Paperback sourcebooks in
The Jossey-Bass Higher Education Series

Jossey-Bass Inc., Publishers
San Francisco • London

Arlene Fingeret, Paul Jurmo (eds.).
*Participatory Literacy Education.*
New Directions for Continuing Education, no. 42.
San Francisco: Jossey-Bass, 1989.

**New Directions for Continuing Education**
Ralph G. Brockett, *Editor-in-Chief*
Alan B. Knox, *Consulting Editor*

**New Directions for Continuing Education** is published quarterly
by Jossey-Bass Inc., Publishers (publication number USPS 493-930).
Second-class postage paid at San Francisco, California, and at
additional mailing offices. POSTMASTER: Send address changes to
Jossey-Bass Inc., Publishers, 350 Sansome Street, San Francisco,
California 94104.

**Editorial correspondence** should be sent to the Editor-in-Chief,
Ralph G. Brockett, Dept. of Technological and Adult Education,
University of Tennessee, 402 Claxton Addition, Knoxville, Tennessee
37996-3400.

Library of Congress Catalog Card Number LC 85-644750

International Standard Serial Number ISSN 0195-2242

International Standard Book Number ISBN 1-55542-861-4

Cover art by WILLI BAUM

Manufactured in the United States of America. Printed on acid-free paper.

# *Ordering Information*

The paperback sourcebooks listed below are published quarterly and can be ordered either by subscription or single copy.

Subscriptions cost $52.00 per year for institutions, agencies, and libraries. Individuals can subscribe at the special rate of $39.00 per year *if payment is by personal check.* (Note that the full rate of $52.00 applies if payment is by institutional check, even if the subscription is designated for an individual.) Standing orders are accepted.

Single copies are available at $12.95 when payment accompanies order. (California, New Jersey, New York, and Washington, D.C., residents please include appropriate sales tax.) For billed orders, cost per copy is $12.95 plus postage and handling.

Substantial discounts are offered to organizations and individuals wishing to purchase bulk quantities of Jossey-Bass sourcebooks. Please inquire.

Please note that these prices are for the calendar year 1989 and are subject to change without notice. Also, some titles may be out of print and therefore not available for sale.

To ensure correct and prompt delivery, all orders must give either the *name of an individual* or an *official purchase order number.* Please submit your order as follows:

*Subscriptions:* specify series and year subscription is to begin.
*Single Copies:* specify sourcebook code (such as, CE1) and first two words of title.

Mail orders for United States and Possessions, Latin America, Canada, Japan, Australia, and New Zealand to:
Jossey-Bass Inc., Publishers
350 Sansome Street
San Francisco, California 94104

Mail orders for all other parts of the world to:
Jossey-Bass Limited
28 Banner Street
London EC1Y 8QE

*New Directions for Continuing Education Series*
Ralph G. Brockett, *Editor-in-Chief*
Alan B. Knox, *Consulting Editor*

CE1    *Enhancing Proficiencies of Continuing Educators,* Alan B. Knox
CE2    *Programming for Adults Facing Mid-Life Change,* Alan B. Knox
CE3    *Assessing the Impact of Continuing Education,* Alan B. Knox

# Contents

# Editors' Notes

Our society makes far more demands for literacy than any other in history. Unfortunately, the number of persons whose skills do not enable them to participate fully as literate members of our literate society is very large. The limits of their literacy skills create obstacles for the development of robust, positive self-images, employment mobility, and full participation in civic and community activities.

Literacy education has become a priority for policy makers who are concerned about maintaining a competitive economy as well as for citizens who are concerned about the basic quality of life for everyone. There is widespread agreement that literacy programs must reach a far larger number of persons than they have been able to reach in the past. However, most of the present programs are constrained by their underlying philosophy, which does not give learners a voice in the conduct of the program. The effectiveness of these programs will be limited because they separate learners from their knowledge and isolate them from their communities, the source of their wisdom and strength.

Participatory literacy education has emerged as an alternative. The participatory program model shares the power equally among learners and staff. It includes a wide range of practices, but all participatory literacy programs have in common that learners have substantial amounts of control, responsibility, and reward vis-à-vis program decision making and operations. The students' knowledge, skills, and experience are valued and respected and provide the foundation upon which further learning is built.

Participatory literacy education programs are presently in the minority in the literacy field, although interest is growing. Because the model requires changing established power relationships, it is often viewed as threatening. It requires a difficult process of organizational renewal and change for programs established in the traditional mode. But we believe that adoption of the model described here is essential if we are to make a substantial impact on the basic literacy skills of adults in the United States. The choice is ours.

The programs highlighted by case studies in this volume provide examples of the emerging theory in action. In some cases, such as the Academy, the program has been participatory from the outset. In others, like those at Literacy Volunteers of New York City and the Center for Literacy in Philadelphia, students and staff have been involved in a transition that has often been difficult. Their words help us to develop insight into some of the basic organizational and personal development

1

issues that must be confronted, particularly in relation to the distribution of power.

This volume provides a framework for thinking about learner participation in adult literacy education programs, case studies of programs that have made active learner involvement central to a variety of practices, and recommendations aimed at further development of the participatory approach as a major force within the adult literacy field in the United States. The contents are grouped in three sections.

The first section provides an introduction, historical context, and conceptual framework for understanding participatory literacy practices. In Chapter One, Arlene Fingeret establishes the historical context within which participatory programs emerged as an alternative to the traditional approaches. She shows how current research and critical analysis seriously undermine the stereotype of nonreading adults as unable to participate as partners in programs.

In Chapter Two, Paul Jurmo provides a theoretical framework for considerations of participation. Jurmo breaks participation down into levels. At the lowest level, students simply come to programs. At the highest level, students have significant amounts of control, responsibility, and reward in relation to program governance and the instructional process. Participatory literacy education aims for the highest level of learner participation, at which power is most fully shared. Jurmo identifies efficiency, personal development, and social change as the major arguments supporting this high level of student involvement.

In the second section, four case studies describe participatory literacy education in practice and illustrate the process through which programs develop these practices. Jurmo begins the section with an introduction that describes the range of practices presently found in programs across the country. In Chapter Four, Raúl Lorenzo Añorve describes the programs of California Literacy. Añorve places the emphasis on workplace efforts, which are especially challenging because employers as well as workers must be involved. California Literacy also provides an example of participatory English-as-a-second-language programming.

Marilyn Boutwell's case study in Chapter Five provides insight into the personal and organizational development processes that accompany the transition from traditional to participatory practice in instruction as well as in program management. In Chapter Six, Susan Lytle, Alisa Belzer, Katherine Schultz, and Marie Vannozzi describe their process of collaboration on two levels. University researchers collaborated with literacy practitioners to develop collaborative assessment practices involving program staff and students. The stages of their work illuminate the difficulties of collaboration across types of institutions as well as the dynamic development of new approaches to assessment. Chapter Seven presents a case study by Rena Soifer, Deborah Young, and Martha Irwin of the

Eastern Michigan University Academy, a program developed through a collaboration of literacy educators, labor unions, and industrial management. The authors argue that it is possible to develop a participatory program while working within industry, and they share some of the experiences they had in struggling to learn how to do so.

The programs described in these case studies are at the forefront of participatory literacy education. There are other outstanding programs that could not be included in this volume because of space limitations. Nevertheless, the number remains small. These programs, and their students and staff, are real leaders. We appreciate their willingness to share their experience and what they have learned.

The chapters in section three provide an overview of existing resources and recommendations for the future based on an analysis of the field and the case studies in section two. In Chapter Eight, Jurmo writes that community-based literacy and volunteer organizations have demonstrated greater leadership in developing participatory practices than have government-funded adult basic education and other literacy programs. He describes the extent of these organizations' participatory efforts and the support they have received from funders, policy makers, and others.

In Chapter Nine, Jurmo presents recommendations for literacy educators, learners, and policy makers. He argues that collaboration must take place on many levels and that policy must be developed to support learners and staff working together as partners. We must continue developing theory to guide our efforts, and we must be realistic about the economic, cultural, bureaucratic, and political constraints under which participatory programs operate. Participatory programs must always be aware of the potential for manipulation, and they must continue to confront the challenges inherent in developing new power relationships. Ongoing research and development and training and networking systems are urgently needed. Development of a base of material and human resources is another priority.

We hope that the materials presented in this volume will clarify these new developments in literacy education and inspire continued dedication to participatory principles. We believe that literacy educators must work together with students as partners if we are to move forward as a society committed to literacy for all.

Arlene Fingeret
Paul Jurmo
Editors

**4**

*Arlene Fingeret is associate professor of adult and community college education at North Carolina State University and director of the North Carolina Center for Literacy Development in Raleigh.*

*Paul Jurmo is senior program associate at the Business Council for Effective Literacy, a national literacy clearinghouse in New York City.*

*Participatory literacy education is based on the belief that*
*learners should be at the center of literacy instruction.*

# The Social and Historical Context of Participatory Literacy Education

*Arlene Fingeret*

Participatory literacy education is a philosophy as well as a set of practices. It is based on the belief that learners—their characteristics, aspirations, backgrounds, and needs—should be at the center of literacy
instruction. This belief implies that the relationship among learners and
program staff is collaborative. The traditional literacy education model
places skills at the center and implies a hierarchical relationship between
educators (who know the skills) and students (who "need" to learn the
skills). Thus, learners in participatory efforts help to define, create, and
maintain the program; those in traditional programs are merely asked to
receive it. Adult educators in traditional programs sometimes claim that
they begin from where the student is. However, even when information
is solicited from students, the power in the program is not shared.

Traditional literacy programs represent our inheritance from a long
history of educational programs designed to socialize students into a
variety of roles in the mainstream society. This chapter begins with an
overview of the history of literacy programs in the United States. The
focus is on students' roles in these programs. Further, the traditional
model has assumed that students are unable to be anything other than

A. Fingeret and P. Jurmo (eds.). *Participatory Literacy Education.*
New Directions for Continuing Education, no. 42. San Francisco: Jossey-Bass, Summer 1989.

recipients of services. Development of a new, learner-centered paradigm must be based on the understanding that students are capable of a wide range of roles inside and outside the literacy program context. Thus, this chapter concludes by examining the traditional view of the characteristics of students and presenting theoretical arguments and empirical evidence that support a more potent view of learners.

## Saving Students and Democracy

We have inherited a largely missionary approach to literacy education that was forged in the Reformation and imported to colonial America. In this conception of literacy education, literacy has been seen both as an instrumental skill and as a moral transforming force that, by enabling an individual to read the Bible, gives the individual access to salvation. From this perspective, the inability to read can be perceived as an indicator of more serious deficits, including a lack of moral development or a propensity for sin. For most of the past two hundred years, teachers have been viewed as missionaries responsible for teaching moral lessons as well as reading skills. Students were the objects of instruction, to be transformed in the crucible of school.

The focus of literacy instruction changed periodically to reflect social conditions, but the purposes of programs, the standards of literacy, and the content of the curriculum have consistently been defined by "experts" rather than by learners. In the early 1800s, education was seen as a tool for unifying the nation; the common moral lessons expressed in primers were expected to provide a basis for shared values (Smith, 1934). The late 1800s saw concern with industrialization, and reading teachers were told that they had to teach what to read as well as how to read to ensure proper moral development. The influx of immigrants in the late 1800s and early 1900s led to a concern with the "purity" of America, and literacy education was once again called on to socialize adults to mainstream norms and values (Graff, 1979).

During World War I, the Armed Services were concerned with the large number of recruits who were unable to read for information or to follow directions. This concern stimulated the development of psychometric testing, which formalized the use of external norms to judge literacy levels and inform instruction (Resnick and Resnick, 1977). Public analysis of the causes of illiteracy shifted from personal moral failure to poor public schools and unenforced compulsory education laws, but literacy retained its connections with the realm of moral action. Illiteracy was identified with ignorance and the inability to be "scientific"; leaders claimed that illiteracy threatened the nation's future industrial development and, more fundamentally, our democracy (McKenny [1925], 1966).

When we entered World War II, concerns about illiteracy reemerged.

The emphasis continued to be on functional problems (for example, recruits could not use written instructional manuals) and on moral issues (for example, nonreading recruits were presumed to be vulnerable to Fascist propaganda). When it became clear that the military had to accept a certain number of nonreading recruits, it developed its own literacy program. However, the military did not want to be responsible for providing continuing adult literacy education. A series of reports released after the war encouraged public action (Caliver, 1951; Ginzberg and Bray, 1953).

The major thrust of these reports was that illiteracy was a threat to democracy because it created vulnerable citizens and undependable soldiers. For example, Goldberg (1951, p. 287) argues that "our millions of illiterate and uninformed citizens constitute a major source of marginally adjusted individuals and are fair game for demagogues." Illiteracy became a topic of concern at the international level as well, where it was connected with "modernization" and development agendas.

During this period, policy makers here and abroad began to talk about "eradicating" illiteracy. The notion of illiteracy as a "disease" gained prominence, as Levine (1982, p. 252) explains: "The prevailing orthodoxy in educational and diplomatic circles [in the 1950s] held illiteracy to be a kind of cultural pathogen analogous to smallpox or malaria and, like them, susceptible to complete eradication. The preferred treatment was the general administration of primary schooling in a more or less standardized form."

American literacy educators of the 1960s and 1970s existed within the broader social constructs of the Great Society and the War on Poverty. Social scientists were writing about disadvantaged and deprived adults, and adult basic educators embraced the prevailing social science models without much critical analysis. Illiterate adults were described as living in a state of psychological and economic poverty; they were seen as lacking the qualities of character as well as the skills necessary for social mobility or economic stability.

Federal legislation of the 1960s was a response to civil unrest as well as to international pressures. Cuba's well-publicized literacy campaign in 1961 fueled Cold War paranoia, and civil rights and anti-Viet Nam War protests fed fears of internal collapse. The disease model had to share time with a "war" model in which illiteracy was to be "attacked" and "combatted." Programs were concerned with shoring up the system and getting marginal adults to fit in or be mainstreamed.

White middle-class norms provided the framework within which literacy programs developed goals of changing students' attitudes and culture as well as teaching literacy skills. This attention to cultural change was not limited to attitudes or values pertaining to literacy. It extended to all areas of adults' lives, including childrearing, marriage, nutrition, personal hygiene, housekeeping, cooking, citizenship, and employment. For example, E. Smith (1968, p. 76) wrote for literacy teachers: "[Adult basic education] aims at bringing the adult basic education student off his social reservation. It aims not at preserving his culture but at changing his culture."

The developing concept of functional literacy quickly became identified with a relatively narrow goal: reading and writing skills sufficient for getting and keeping a job. In the 1970s, the goal was extended to the acquisition of "life skills," "coping skills," or "survival skills." The resulting programs continued to be designed to teach students how to fit into mainstream society, as Thompson (1983, p. 44) asserts when describing "coping skills" curricula: "The emphasis is on training and treatment and adjusting rather than on consciousness-raising, critical awareness, and the pursuit of political and social change." As Johnson (1985, p. 14) explains, "The attitude here is that the most literacy education can do is provide the hard-to-reach with the 'coping' skills necessary for survival rather than with sufficient skills to enable them to take control of their lives."

Competency-based adult literacy education emerged in the 1970s. Theoretically, students can play a major role in defining the competencies that they want to achieve and the way in which they will do so. In practice, competency-based programs tend to judge adults' existing skills by a predefined list that reflects the activities deemed most necessary for those whose goal is to live among or be subservient to the middle class and to conduct their lives as the middle class thinks it is correct for them to conduct their lives.

In the 1980s, most programs continue to be based on a model in which the educators make decisions and expect students to conform. Today we hear that literacy education is important because it supports the position of the United States in the world economic order and because it enables workers to keep pace with developing technology and increasing literacy demands in their workplaces. This rationale continues to support the notion that literacy programs are designed to meet the needs of those in power. The curriculum continues to be created on the basis of experts' views of the demands of the environment, not by working with students to reflect their lives and concerns. Students continue to be viewed as objects who are to be recruited, retained, and taught in organizations that have been created by others and that others maintain.

To summarize: We imported from Western Europe and kept alive a tradition that viewed literacy skills as both functionally important and necessary for moral development. The standards of functioning consistently have been set externally to learners, whether by the church, the military, the corporation, or the schools. The assumptions of undeveloped moral fiber, character, and skills lead to a notion of nonreading adults as incompetent and needing help on the one hand or as needing salvation on the other. This tradition also suggests that the rest of society has to be protected from these adults, who threaten the future of the United States.

Literacy education is organized to teach the skills determined by educators and others in power, not by educators and learners acting collaboratively. Indeed, learners have not been included to any large extent in any of the conversations about the purposes or goals of programs, the curriculum, or the basis for evaluation.

It is in this context that participatory programs can be understood as providing an alternative. With their emphasis on sharing power with learners and their fundamental assumption that students are capable of participating as partners in programs, they challenge the prevailing conventional wisdom and practices.

## Images of Learners

The image of nonreading adults as fundamentally incompetent is deeply embedded in conventional wisdom. Many educators say that participatory practices are theoretically appealing but impractical because nonreading adults are not capable of participating more actively in programs. It is important to address this point by examining the assumptions that have been made about the characteristics of nonreading adults, because recent research and new theoretical interpretations call the old conventional wisdom into question.

*Dignity.* Foremost, it is important to recognize that nonreading adults are the creators of their own social lives, as imperfect as those lives may appear by middle-class standards. They participate in the ongoing creation and maintenance of the social world in which they live. Their inherent dignity is at the heart of the belief that they are not only able but that it is their right to participate in creating programs that are supposed to serve their interests (Fingeret, 1982).

*Diversity.* It is also important to understand that nonreading adults are not a homogeneous group. In fact, the population of adults with low literacy skill levels is diverse, and it includes a large number of persons who have been consistently productive workers, family members, and in some cases community leaders. Reder and Green (1985, pp. 7-8), who have conducted numerous research studies with nonreading adults, claim that "stereotyped ideas about 'functionally illiterate' adults, such as their being unable to read at all, or not having useful skills and being unable to cope in daily life (other than being able to 'hide' their illiteracy from others), or being ignorant about most matters, or unable to participate in most of society's activities . . . have little empirical validity."

*Intelligence.* It is also important to confront the assumption that nonreading adults were schooling "failures" and that they therefore do not have the intelligence that it takes to participate meaningfully in program processes. This assumption ignores the fact that many nonreading adults have not attended schools or that they have attended only sporadically. More fundamentally, however, numerous studies document the fact that intelligence and success in school do not necessarily coincide. Intelligence test bias, educational system cultural bias, and environmental and economic circumstances often militate against successful performance of school tasks.

The intellectual ability of nonreading adults is doubted also because literacy is viewed as a key to the development of higher-order intellectual ability. For example, Wallace (1965, p. 9), in a widely used training handbook, summarized the view that many continue to hold: "The mind of an illiterate person is like an unplanted seed. Inside the shell, there is the germ of life waiting to be awakened and quickened."

Scribner and Cole (1978) label this approach to the characteristics of nonreading adults a *developmental framework*. They claim that "its presuppositions implicitly or explicitly inform the great majority of literacy . . . programs" (Scribner and Cole, 1978, p. 445), and they explain (p. 451) that the developmental perspective "specifies literacy's effects as the emergence of general mental capacities—abstract thinking, for example, or logical operations—rather than specific skills. These abilities are presumed to characterize the individual's intellectual functioning across a wide range of tasks. . . . From this perspective, the capacities generated by literacy are seen not merely as different but as higher-order capacities because they resemble the abilities that psychological theories attribute to later stages in development." However, "research does not support designing literacy programs on the assumption that nonliterates do not think abstractly, do not reason logically, or lack other basic mental processes" (Scribner and Cole, 1978, p. 459).

Prevailing classroom practices propagate the stereotype of the incompetent nonreader since "in [formal] classrooms it is easy to maintain the unequal power relations between teacher and learner that nurture the stereotype of the adult literacy student as low in self-esteem, reluctant to take risks, and concerned whether to use English correctly or not at all" (Weber, 1975, p. 246).

Unfortunately, the research is often conducted in precisely these classrooms, and then the findings are generalized to adults with low reading skill levels. Such research ignores the limitations created by observing or interviewing adults in settings in which they are made to feel powerless. It is as if researchers cannot imagine that these students have a life outside the literacy program or that literacy is not central to that life.

In contrast to the prevailing trend, Heath (1980) studied the functions of language and literacy in two working-class communities. She claims that "learners frequently possess and display in out-of-school contexts skills relevant to using literacy which are not effectively exploited in school learning environments" (Heath, 1980, p. 132).

*Culture.* The culture of nonreading adults has been judged within the normative framework of the dominant group's cultural patterns. However, it is possible to try to understand different cultural patterns on their own terms. Such research as that of Fingeret (1983), Reder (1987), Reder and Green (1985), and Heath (1980) provides examples of the rich understanding that we can develop when we are open to learning from nonreading adults about their lives.

For example, Fingeret (1983) conducted a study of nonreading adults in their communities. She proposes that we think of adults who do not read as members of primarily oral subcultures, not as nonfunctioning members of the dominant literate culture. The oral subculture is rooted in concrete experience. Talk is at the heart of the oral subculture, and talk requires consistent face-to-face interaction. Members of oral subcultures value spending time together for learning, sharing information, and providing mutual assistance. This fundamental cultural characteristic is at odds with the prevailing assumption that nonreading adults are socially isolated, alienated, and inarticulate. It suggests that interaction is central to daily life but that it follows "rules" that are different from the rules of the classroom. Students are often made to feel that their culture does not support literacy development, and their rich patterns of social interaction are not viewed as resources appropriate to the instructional setting.

All adults participate in a community of close friends, family members, neighbors, and sometimes coworkers. Each adult always has an inner group consisting of the persons with whom he or she has consistent contact and from whom he or she derives a sense of mutual respect and sharing. Nonreading adults find assistance with reading and writing tasks from the members of their communities, and they in turn offer help with other tasks or information. For example, nonreading adults may provide assistance with child care, insight into the politics of the welfare system, or knowledge about how to fix a car in exchange for help in reading a letter or filling out a form. When this exchange process is viewed as mutually beneficial, nonreading adults see themselves as contributing members of their communities.

Reder (1987) describes different types of knowledge that community members bring to a literacy task. These types include "technological knowledge"—the actual skills with reading and writing. Other members bring "functional knowledge"—an understanding of the relationship between the message and the way in which it is presented (for example, form letter, business letter). Still others contribute "social knowledge"—an understanding of the meaning that the literacy act has in a specific situation.

Of course, the exchange processes in a community also include skills and knowledge that have no relation to literacy. As long as nonreading adults are able to see their own contributions to the community's pool of skills and knowledge, they feel that they participate as equals. They see themselves as interdependent. It is only in the larger literacy society that the inability to read defines them as unequal and incompetent (deAvila, 1983).

When culture is viewed on its own terms as the foundation for learning, an asset brought to the teaching-learning interaction, not as a set of "bad" behaviors that have to be changed, nonreading adults can be viewed as able collaborators in literacy programming. Moreover, the responsibility of programs to work with learners as collaborators becomes clear as learners are seen as competent adults functioning in a milieu for which literacy is not central. The participation of learners in programs then is understood in terms of cross-cultural communication and mutual learning and negotiation.

*Collaboration.* The oral subculture exists in tension with the larger literate society. As mentioned earlier, nonreading adults work out ways of dealing with society's reading and writing demands. Research rejects the conventional wisdom that nonreading adults are social isolates and supports our understanding that nonreading adults engage in many modes of collaboration and cooperation. In fact, literacy practices are often collaborative, as the research of Reder (1987) and Reder and Green (1985) has shown.

According to Reder (1987), literacy practices that regularly involve more than one person can be described as *collaborative.* This may mean that two or more persons engage in reading tasks together, such as responsive reading in church, or it may mean that one person does the actual reading or writing while other persons actively manipulate the information involved. In particular, Reder (1987) identifies practices as *scribal* when one person who has the technical writing skills collaborates with others who have the knowledge or status to do such a task as writing a letter or filling out a form.

This notion provides not only another way of understanding literacy practices in communities, but it also points out that learners bring skills in collaboration and that these skills are connected with their experience of literacy. However, Reder (1987) points out that in the larger society the roles in collaborative literacy practices are often connected not with proficiency in literacy tasks but with personal status. For example, a secretary is not necessarily a better reader or writer than his or her employer. Reder argues that this fact has one important implication: "If social factors strongly influence individuals' access to participant roles that have specialized responsibilities for reading and writing and if experience in those roles is closely linked to developing a particular body of knowledge and skills, then those same social factors will influence the social distribution of skills and knowledge within the participant community. Increasing individuals' comfort with or access to roles having specialized responsibilities for reading or writing may stimulate the development of the requisite skills and knowledge" (Reder, 1987, p. 8). Thus, participatory literacy programs that provide access to new roles have potential for enhancing learning directly as well as for building on students' experience and strengths.

Of course, it is important to remember that solitary literacy activities are highly valued by schools and other Western institutions. But research conducted by Reder (1987) and others forces us to recognize that literacy as a social practice involving more than one person in a collaborative effort is extensive.

*Aspirations and Resistance.* Finally, we must recognize that nonreading adults often make the choice not to participate in literacy programs. Rather than being unmotivated, or having low aspirations, or being afraid of more failure, these adults often have decided that school has failed them. They identify costs with returning to school; it disrupts their communities, and it isolates them. These costs may be more than nonreading adults are willing to pay when the curriculum appears to be irrelevant to their lives.

Nonreading adults often can be viewed as resisters rather than as failures in the educational system. Quigley (1987) examined resisters' responses to the values and culture of schooling as well as the curriculum. He found that resisters were intolerant of the values and culture being imposed on them but that they did not resist developing the actual skills of reading and writing. Quigley's work supports the findings of other researchers that nonreading adults would like to know how to read but that they have been unwilling to tolerate the profoundly disrespectful environment of most educational programs. Holzman (1986, p. 32) reminds us that "all too often the organization of literacy education, of schooling in general, in this country is at the service of institutional or bureaucratic rather than human priorities."

## Conclusion

No reliable evidence supports the contention that nonreading adults are unable to share power in literacy education programs. Nonreading adults are a diverse group of persons with a range of personality characteristics, skills, knowledge, and aspirations. They usually have had little experience with the processes used to operate educational programs. Moreover, their class status may have made it difficult for them to develop a belief in their own ability to participate in governance of formalized instruction. At the same time, program staff have often not viewed

14

learners' culture on its own terms. They often do not recognize the strengths that students bring to the program or the culturally related nature of program and instructional tasks. Thus, participatory literacy education should be viewed as a process of cross-cultural communication, negotiation, and mutual learning.

## References

Caliver, A. "Illiteracy and Manpower Mobilization." *School Life,* 1951, *33,* 131.

deAvila, M. "Illiterate Adults and Readers: Their Exchange System." *Adult Literacy and Basic Education,* 1983, 7 (3), 117-128.

Fingeret, A. "The Illiterate Underclass: Demythologizing an American Stigma." Unpublished doctoral dissertation, Syracuse University, 1982.

Fingeret, A. "Social Network: A New Perspective on Independence and Illiterate Adults." *Adult Education Quarterly,* 1983, *33,* 133-146.

Ginzberg, E., and Bray, D. W. *The Uneducated.* New York: Columbia University Press, 1953.

Goldberg, S. *Army Training of Illiterates in World War II.* New York: Teachers College, Columbia University, 1951.

Graff, H. *The Literacy Myth: Literacy and Social Structure in the Nineteenth Century City.* Orlando, Fla.: Academic Press, 1979.

Heath, S. B. "The Functions and Uses of Literacy." *Journal of Communication,* 1980, *30* (1), 123-133.

Holzman, M. "Opinion: The Social Context of Literacy Education." *College English,* 1986, *48* (1), 27-33.

Johnson, J. N. *Adults in Crisis: Illiteracy in America.* San Francisco: National Adult Literacy Project, Far West Laboratory, and the NETWORK, Inc., 1985.

Levine, K. "Functional Literacy: Fond Illusions and False Economies." *Harvard Educational Review,* 1982, *52* (3), 249-266.

McKenny, C. "An Illiteracy Program." In F. Lanning and W. Many, *Basic Education for the Disadvantaged Adult.* New York: Houghton Mifflin, 1966. (Originally published 1925.)

Quigley, A. "The Resisters: An Analysis of Nonparticipation in Adult Basic Education." Paper presented at the Adult Education Research Conference, Laramie, Wyoming, May 1987.

Reder, S. M. "Comparative Aspects of Functional Literacy Development: Three Ethnic Communities." In D. Wagner (ed.), *The Future of Literacy in a Changing World.* Vol. 1. Oxford, England: Pergamon Press, 1987.

Reder, S. M., and Green, K. R. *Giving Literacy Away.* Portland, Oreg.: Literacy and Language Program, Northwest Regional Laboratory, 1985. (ED 253 775)

Resnick, D. P., and Resnick, L. B. "The Nature of Literacy: An Historical Exploration." *Harvard Educational Review,* 1977, *47,* 370-385.

Scribner, S., and Cole, M. "Literacy Without Schooling: Testing for Intellectual Effects." *Harvard Educational Review,* 1978, *48,* 448-466.

Smith, E. H. "Background of Literacy Education." In I. R. Jahns and H. C. Brady, Jr. (eds.), *The Adult Basic Education Curriculum and Its Development.* Tallahassee: Department of Adult Education, Florida State University, 1968.

Smith, N. B. *American Reading Instruction.* New York: Silver Burdett, 1934.

Thompson, J. L. "Adult Education and the Disadvantaged." *Convergence,* 1983, *16* (2), 42-47.

Wallace, M. C. *Literacy Instructors' Handbook.* Chicago: Follett, 1965.

Weber, R. "Adult Illiteracy in the United States." In J. B. Carroll and J. Chall (eds.), *Toward a Literate Society*. New York: McGraw-Hill, 1975.

*Arlene Fingeret is associate professor of adult and community college education at North Carolina State University and director of the North Carolina Center for Literacy Development in Raleigh.*

*Active learner participation in adult literacy programs enables learners to take higher degrees of control, responsibility, and reward vis-à-vis program activities. Active participation can improve program efficiency, enhance learners' personal development, and enable them to transform the larger social contexts in which they live.*

# The Case for Participatory Literacy Education

*Paul Jurmo*

The preceding chapter established that adults with low levels of basic skills are capable of participating actively in literacy programs and other social contexts. We need now to examine what it means to participate actively in a literacy program. This chapter, which is based on Chapter Two of Jurmo (1987), addresses that issue.

## What Is Active Learner Participation?

When learners and practitioners are asked what active learner participation is, a wide range of answers results. Participation varies from simple attendance to active control of one or more program activities.

If these responses are organized according to the amounts of control, reward, and responsibility accorded the learner, several levels of participation emerge. Organized along the steps of a ladder (Arnstein, 1971) with the lowest levels of participation on the bottom rungs and the highest levels at the top, these levels might look as shown in Figure 1.

This chapter is based on Jurmo, 1987, Chapter Two.
The author wishes to thank the Association for Community Based Education for its partial funding of research costs for Chapters Two, Three, Eight, and Nine of this volume.

A. Fingeret and P. Jurmo (eds.). *Participatory Literacy Education.*
New Directions for Continuing Education, no. 42. San Francisco: Jossey-Bass, Summer 1989.

**Figure 1. Levels of Learner Participation in Adult Literacy Programs**

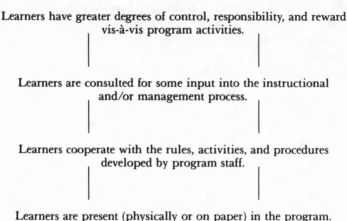

Learners have greater degrees of control, responsibility, and reward vis-à-vis program activities.

Learners are consulted for some input into the instructional and/or management process.

Learners cooperate with the rules, activities, and procedures developed by program staff.

Learners are present (physically or on paper) in the program.

This hierarchy of levels shows that there is no one simple definition of learner participation. In some instances, a learner participates merely by signing up for a program and showing up for a minimal number of classes. In its most active form, participation means that the learner has active control, responsibility, and reward vis-à-vis some or all program activities.

It is these highest levels of learner participation for which advocates of participatory education generally aim. In practice, literacy programs aiming at the highest levels of learner participation give learners ongoing opportunities to plan and implement a wide range of instructional and management activities within the program. While it is impossible for all learners to be actively involved in all activities all the time, maintaining a high average level of participation is the goal.

**Why Is Active Learner Participation Important in Instruction?**

The arguments for the importance of active learner participation can be organized according to three major purposes that active learner participation can serve in the instructional process: efficiency, personal development, and social change.

*Efficiency.* A number of researchers have concluded that, for instruction to be successful, learners must be given opportunities to take on highly active roles in making printed language meaningful to themselves and others. This conclusion is based on research on the ways in which fluent readers and writers operate and on the ways in which instruction can facilitate or impede the development of fluent literacy.

Successful readers develop strategies enabling them to relate printed forms of language to what they already know about the content and form of language. In this process, the learner attaches a meaning to the printed language. Successful writers are able to put thought into a printed form that others can relate to their prior experience and develop meaning for.

This view of the reading and writing process is central to the whole-language approach to literacy instruction. Whole-language advocates argue that reading instruction should be organized to maximize the brain's strong point, the "utilization of what it knows already," and minimize the brain's weakest area, which has been identified as the "processing of . . . new information, especially when that new information makes little sense" (Smith, 1978, p. 179).

According to this view, the process of learning to read is one in which the reader gradually makes "sense of more and more kinds of language in more and more contexts," a process that is "fundamentally a matter of experience" (Smith, 1978, p. 191) through which the reader uses skills of selecting, predicting, searching, and tentative choosing (Goodman and Niles, 1970). All these skills require the reader to take an energetic, active role as a seeker of meaning in print. The outcome of this process is someone who can distinguish between the form of printed language and its true function: reading and writing for meaning (Watson, 1979). Reading and writing are "tools which language users use in the process of getting things done" (Harste, Woodward, and Burke, 1984, p. 204).

To facilitate acquisition of these tools, the teacher does not need to rely on one universally applicable instructional method. Instead, the teacher should seek to set up a learning environment that encourages the learner to explore a variety of forms of written language and find the ones that are particularly meaningful (Smith, 1978). These forms of language can include "daily journals, newspapers, message boards, letters to pen pals, recipes, menus, reading environmental print, and other functional uses of written language" (Harste, Woodward, and Burke, 1984, p. 205) all taken from contexts meaningful to the learner (Smith, 1978).

In such a process, readers should be allowed to make mistakes and learn to distinguish between forms of language that help the acquisition of meaning and forms of language that hinder development of meaning. The reader should be allowed to correct himself or herself and not have to depend on others to make the corrections (Smith, 1978). Instructors can facilitate this process by providing "multiple opportunities to test their written language hypotheses in a low-risk environment" (Harste, Woodward, and Burke, 1984, p. 205). When learners in these ways choose and interpret reading experiences freely, they are likely to develop a greater sense of ownership of—and interest in—the reading process. Finally, the reader should not be expected to learn symbols outside a meaningful context.

Unfortunately, most instructional systems are not based on such principles, and teachers often lack the time or resources needed to provide this more ideal learning environment (Smith, 1978). At the least, teachers and others who believe in these principles should strive to limit the conditions (such as presenting learners with meaningless forms of language) that reduce efficient learning.

These and other whole-language arguments (Graves, 1981) are based primarily on research done with school-age children. Others have based similar arguments on research with adult low-level readers.

Proponents of a contextualized view of literacy argue that "illiteracy is situational; it can only be defined in context and can only be tackled in [the] context" in which each individual lives (Harman, 1987, p. 44). This contextualized approach is particularly evident in current employee basic skills efforts in which the context is defined as the workplace in which learners are expected to perform certain literacy tasks. Some workplace programs have been structured so that workers actively discuss and teach each other from reading materials found on the job. They also carry out work-related research projects, collecting information about a particular work procedure by reading manuals or by direct observation and then interpreting that information and recording it in charts, graphs, or written form. This active approach to learning is based on the assumption that workers will find such uses of literacy familiar, meaningful, and motivating. In the process, workers can be expected to enhance their understanding of job tasks while at the same time improving the reading, writing, thinking, teamwork, and verbal communication skills needed on the job (Harman, 1987; Sticht, 1987).

These arguments from the worlds of children's reading research and workplace literacy share the belief that those who provide literacy instruction—whether for children or for adults—must understand how fluent readers and writers acquire meaning from print. Literacy instructors should then build on that understanding to give learners multiple opportunities to develop their own abilities to make sense of printed forms of language.

*Personal Development.* Another set of arguments holds that, although the development in learners of efficient reading and writing skills is desirable, it is not in itself an adequate goal for literacy programs. This second set of arguments claims that, because many learners come to literacy programs lacking in other cognitive and social traits, literacy programs need to be structured to enhance development of those characteristics as well. These other characteristics include critical thinking or problem solving, ability to work collaboratively with others, self-esteem, and interest in continuing one's education.

This perspective on participatory learning argues that such personal qualities are basic to the development of a mature, healthy adult. Without such qualities, the individual is likely to remain passive and not use even the technical skills that he or she already has. The educational process can help the learner to acquire these personal traits by providing the learner with opportunities to set goals, explore options, and develop strategies for meeting goals through active experimentation. In these ways, active learner participation in the educational process is seen as central to achievement of these important personal goals.

This perspective is found in the work of humanistic educators who argue that education should aim at helping the learner to develop skills of inquiry that enable the individual (with or without the help of others) to take the initiative in a self-directed learning process. Learners should be able to assess their own learning needs and objectives, identify human and material resources, and develop, implement, and evaluate appropriate learning strategies (Knowles, 1975).

According to this view, the learner should no longer be seen as a mere object to be shaped by the educational process. Rather, the learner must become "the subject of his own education," no longer "submitting to education" but instead "educating himself" (Faure and others, 1972, p. 161).

These humanistic educators argue that a "theoretically optimal experience of personal growth," whether in the form of "client-centered therapy or some other experience of learning," would enable an individual to "function in all [his or her] complexity" and actively chart the course of his or her life (Rogers, 1969, p. 288). One such educator (Curran, 1976) developed a group-learning approach that "aims at adapting basic subtleties and awareness from the field of counseling and psychotherapy and integrating them into learning" (p. 1). Curran's group-learning approach aims at developing "a very special kind of community involvement . . . and a kind of security and support" among all members of the group. This mutual support is seen as the opposite of the isolation created by "competitive, 'laissez-faire' classroom individualism" (Curran, 1976, p. 1). A supportive atmosphere of this type allows the learner to advance from an initial stage of dependence on the teacher to increased self-confidence as an active, independent developer of new knowledge. In addition, the learner becomes more able to help fellow group members to proceed in these ways.

Similar arguments are made by writers who focus on reading and writing instruction per se. These writers argue that literacy instruction must recognize that many learners come to the educational setting with a limited sense of who they are and what they can do with their lives. These learners are in danger of losing their own culture and of becoming nonentities in the dominant society (Ashton-Warner, 1963). For those with such a perspective on life, reading and writing are a ritual in which "appearance" is overemphasized and "meaning is atrophied" (Ashton-Warner, 1963, p. 176).

To counteract these destructive tendencies, educators need to develop reading and writing instruction focused on issues that have meaning for the learner. In some cases, these themes might be controversial ones like fear or sex (Ashton-Warner, 1963). Teachers must not shy away from such topics. Rather, they should recognize that many learners have unanswered questions about these kinds of sensitive issues. By dealing constructively with these topics in basic skills sessions, teachers can achieve two goals at the same time: Learners can achieve a deeper understanding of questions of personal concern to themselves, and they can develop their basic skills by using them to achieve personally meaningful goals. Through such personally meaningful uses of language, learners can enhance their self-image and reduce their anxiety levels. Proponents of this approach argue that it succeeds because it "returns teaching to where [learners] *are* and removes it from the esoteric realm of where they *ought* to be" (Fader, 1976, p. 163). In contrast, poor readers have only been "taught the elements—the pieces—of reading," not the "why" (Fader, 1976, p. 192).

*Social Change.* Still another line of thought holds that efficiency and personal development are worthy goals but that they do not go far enough in getting at the fundamental causes of the problems faced by most undereducated adults. Advocates of social change claim that, to understand those problems, we must study the historical conditions that shape an illiterate adult's life. In the case of a large segment of the adult nonreaders in the United States, life has been characterized by poor physical conditions, poor-quality education, inferior social status, and a lack of economic and political power.

Supporters of the social-change analysis argue that it is not a coincidence that many nonreaders live in oppressive conditions. Their illiteracy is a direct result of the conditions, and there is little chance that the cycle of illiteracy within oppressed populations will be broken unless the conditions are eliminated. It is the job of adult education to enable learners to participate actively in changing those conditions.

Such an educational process aimed at social change provides opportunities in which learners actively analyze and shape tasks facing them in the program. The learner thereby learns by doing. He or she learns to take an active role in transforming the world outside by developing the needed abilities within the educational program setting. This approach requires a collective effort of learners and educators working in a two-way, dialogical relationship to analyze and change the status quo. It is therefore inherently political and a step beyond the more individually oriented personal development approach. To a large degree, this perspective springs from adult literacy efforts in the Third World. Brazilian educator Paulo Freire (1985) is a central figure among those who have considered the implications of literacy education for social change, and literacy efforts worldwide are being built on ideas borrowed from his work.

His writing articulates the basic premises of the social-change perspective. For example, he argues that illiteracy is neither a disease that needs to be cured nor a poisonous herb that needs to be eradicated. It is rather "one of the concrete expressions of an unjust social reality. . . . [It is] not strictly a linguistic or exclusively pedagogical or methodological problem. It is political. . . . Literacy [is] . . . a process of search and creation . . . to perceive the deeper meaning of language and the word, the word that, in essence, they are being denied" (Freire, 1985, p. 10).

The role of learners in such education is to identify themes of personal importance to themselves, to develop their own texts based on those themes, and to critically analyze texts produced by others. Through this process of dialogue among learners and educational facilitators, both learners and practitioners become creative subjects able to identify the problems within their situations and find solutions for those problems. This process is to form the basis for the individual or collective action needed to produce positive changes in the situations in which the learners live.

Freire (1985, p. 137) sees those who focus on personal development as the goal of literacy instruction as limited by their inability or unwillingness to go beyond individualized—and hence incremental—change: "Even though they speak of liberating education, they are conditioned by their vision of liberation as an individual activity that should take place through a change of consciousness and not through the social and historical praxis of human beings." Education is thus to be seen as part of a large process of change, not as a mere fine-tuning of the individual's outlook and technical skills.

United States–based educator Carman St. John Hunter (1987, pp. 4–7) analyzes the causes of the illiteracy problem and what must be done to solve it: "Illiteracy is not an isolated phenomenon. It can neither be understood nor responded to apart from the complex set of social, political, and economic issues of which it is but one indicator. . . . Poverty is the underlying cause of illiteracy. Without any proven will or ability to break the chains of poverty, no government has been able to make significant progress toward universal literacy. . . . Literacy cannot be understood as a remedial program designed and delivered by zealous missionaries to those 'in need.' Rather, literacy levels will increase where there is serious commitment to goals of equity and justice and where the educationally disadvantaged are able to be involved in shaping their own learning within the context of reshaping the social, political, economic, and cultural environment within which they live. If we are to begin with programs that promote participation and direction by learners, that degree of openness can become a first step toward the larger, more socially and economically inclusive change that will provide the basis on which universal literacy can be realized."

Supporters in the United States of this social-change approach call for a shift in the nation's literacy efforts toward a new emphasis on learner-centered goals. In this approach, learners determine program goals and strategies and teach and otherwise help each other in various aspects of the program (Fox, 1986). Social-change practitioners have built curricula around such learner-identified themes as marriage and child-rearing, sexuality, self-government, utopia, school experiences, clothing styles, and even *the hamburger*—a code word for the fast-food industry (Shor, 1980). In participatory leaning activities, learners work together to explore these issues and determine how they would deal with them in the real world. Such activities are seen as a means of counteracting the negative effects of schooling and mass media on the learners' self-image and world outlook. As one proponent of this approach explains, "A pedagogy which empowers students to intervene in the making of history is more than a literacy campaign. Critical education prepares students to be their own agents for social change, their own creators of democratic culture" (Shor, 1980, p. 48).

## Why Is Active Learner Participation Important in Program Management?

Most of the literature on learner-centered literacy education focuses on the active roles that learners can play in the instructional process. But much of what goes on in literacy programs is not strictly instructional in nature. Recruitment of new learners, fund raising, public relations, the setting of program policy, staff training, program logistics, and other noninstructional activities provide the framework of resources within which instructional services can be provided.

Historically, program staff operate these management-related activities. But learners have increasingly become involved in the management of their programs. The same general kinds of arguments just cited for learner participation in instruction can be made for active learner participation in management. These arguments are occasionally found in the literature on literacy education, but they are more common in writings on management of for-profit and nonprofit organizations and in the literature on community organizing.

*Efficiency and Personal Development.* Three major reports on effective literacy program practice describe examples of learner participation in various management-related activities (Balmuth, 1987; Lerche, 1985; Mayer, 1984). All three reports argue that such participation increases the efficiency of program operations or enhances the self-esteem and other personal attributes of the learners involved.

For example, current and former literacy students are seen as particularly effective recruiters of new students, as they can "go to areas of need for presentations concerning their own personal success stories" (S. Darling quoted in Balmuth, 1987, p. 5 ). "Word of mouth is at its best when the words are from a 'satisfied customer.' When this customer is a friend, relative, or community resident respected by a potential student, recruitment becomes a self-generating process" (Lerche, 1985, p. 49).

Once new learners have been recruited, veteran learners can help with intake procedures—initial interviews, scheduling, and needs assessments. These early experiences in a program can make or break a newcomer's willingness to stay with the program. Veteran learners can help newcomers make it through this initial "journey on eggshells" (Balmuth, 1987, p. 4).

Buddy systems—in which experienced students serve as mentors to new students—are cited (S. Darling cited in Balmuth, 1987) as useful in reducing dropout rates and absenteeism and in generally maintaining learner morale and interest in the program. The same purposes are achieved by self-help support groups and social activities (P. C. Gold cited in Balmuth, 1987). In such peer-support activities as rap sessions, experienced students "can explain how they deal with the problems and successfully completed the program"; these personal stories "are real and believable and give new students confidence in the claims of program staff" (Lerche, 1985, p. 65).

Learners can make the programs more responsive to their own real needs and interests by serving on program boards of directors and advisory committees, in staff orientation and training, and in program evaluation and goal-setting (Mayer, 1984). Such roles for learners in the planning and evaluation of programs can enhance learner ownership of the program, smooth communications within the program, and clarify learners' interests vis-à-vis staff expectations (Kinsey, 1978).

These forms of learner involvement "build on the fact that adults have already engaged the world, learned a considerable amount, and probably taught someone something" already (Deveaux, 1984, p. 11). Peers-helping-peers minimizes dependency on staff and maximizes group problem solving and "group energy and commitment . . . People who teach others develop confidence, self-reliance, learn to do homework, and come to school regularly" (Deveaux, 1984, p. 11). Peer-help can also have therapeutic value, "for who better than they know" about the problems their fellow learners face (Deveaux, 1984, p. 11).

For one participatory program, learner participation "means having students elect representatives to the program's board of directors, helping students develop committees to help with building maintenance, fund raising, curriculum development, and whatever is appropriate for a program. . . . Such activities as bus trips or theater parties are among the few social events in which adults who cannot read can participate and not have to worry about being exposed as an illiterate because their companions on these outings will be fellow students and staff and all can help one another" (Deveaux, 1984, p. 12).

*Social Change.* As in the case of instruction, a variety of arguments can be made for active learner participation in program management from the social-change perspective. Most of these arguments are found in the literature on socioeconomic development, community organizing, and organizational development. Kindervatter (1979) summarizes these arguments in her survey of efforts to promote sociopolitical empowerment of historically powerless groups. Central to all these empowerment efforts is the active participation of client groups in democratic decision making about the course of those efforts.

For example, critics of current national development efforts argue that the key to the modernization of society is a restructuring of the relationship between government and people. In that new order, the people would have a say in policies that affect their lives. "People can be expected to invest in a modern economy only when they believe they are part of it and can benefit from it" (E. Owens and R. Shaw quoted in Kindervatter, 1979, pp. 42–43). One critical issue in any effort to develop society is the factor of popular control, "the difference between being the agent of one's own development as defined in one's own terms and being a mere beneficiary of development as defined by someone else" (D. Goulet and M. Hudson quoted in Kindervatter, 1979, p. 43).

At the local level, community organizers have recognized the principles of democratic decision making and developed activities and structures in which community members themselves have greater measures of control. These attempts to organize communities to solve local problems "begin with the people's interests . . . move at the community's pace . . . develop 'native' leaders . . . promote peer support and mutual help . . . involve cooperative community problem solving . . . emphasize discussion methods, democratic procedures, and action taking . . . include an organizer who [facilitates rather than dominates the process] . . . and [gradually] transfers initiative and responsibility from the organizer to the people" (Kindervatter, 1979, pp. 87–88).

Efforts to democratize the workplace are sources of similar arguments for participant control. Apart from the material and emotional benefits that accrue to workers from managing—and in some cases owning— their own workplaces, workplace democratization can also enable workers to see that "changes are possible. These skills more than any single change are perhaps the main accomplishment" (D. Zwerdling quoted in Kindervatter, 1979, p. 97). With this altered sense of what they can accomplish through collective analysis and action, workers have a new potential to make changes in the larger society outside.

These approaches to participatory management at the national, local, and workplace levels attempt to "give people power as decision makers, not just 'advisers,' on all aspects of planning, from design to implementation to evaluation . . . base 'content' on people's immediate interests . . . pose problems which participants themselves solve through discussion and action taking . . . utilize methods which promote self-expression and dialogue . . . recognize the importance of training change agents according to the same participatory principles . . . may begin with an imposed structure but gradually enable people to define and control their own structure" (Kindervatter, 1979, p. 137).

These voices from the realms of national development, community organizing, and workplace democratization do not come from the adult literacy field. Nevertheless, they support the notion that client groups can become more politically empowered through participation in the management of the organizations with which they come into contact.

## Conclusion

To participate actively in a literacy program, learners must do more than show up for classes and passively do what they are told. To participate actively, they must take on higher degrees of control, responsibility, and reward vis-à-vis program activities.

Advocates of such active roles for learners argue that active learner participation in instruction and program management can increase program efficiency, enhance learners' personal development, and enable them to transform the larger social contexts in which they live.

## References

Arnstein, S. R. "Eight Rungs on the Ladder of Citizen Participation." In E. S. Cahn and B. A. Passett (eds.), *Citizen Participation: Effecting Community Change*. New York: Praeger, 1971.

Ashton-Warner, S. *Teacher*. New York: Bantam, 1963.

Balmuth, M. *Essential Characteristics of Effective Adult Literacy Programs: A Review and Analysis of the Research*. Albany: Adult Beginning Reader Project, New York State Education Department, 1987.

Curran, C. A. *Counseling-Learning in Second Languages*. Apple River, Ill.: Apple River Press, 1976.

Deveaux, J. "Identifying Target Populations for Adult Literacy Instruction." Paper prepared for the National Adult Literacy Project, May 18, 1984.

Fader, D. *The New Hooked on Books*. New York: Berkley, 1976.

Faure, E., Herrera, F., Kaddoura, A.-R., Lopes, H., Petrovsky, A. V., Rahnema, M., and Ward, F. C. *Learning to Be: The World of Education Today and Tomorrow*. Paris: UNESCO, 1972.

Fox, M. *A Look at Illiteracy in America Today—The Problem, the Solutions, the Alternatives*. Washington, D. C.: Push Literacy Action Now, 1986.

Freire, P. *The Politics of Education*. South Hadley, Mass.: Bergin & Garvey, 1985.

Goodman, K. S., and Niles, O. S. "Behind the Eye: What Happens in Reading." In K. S. Goodman and O. S. Niles (eds.), *Reading Process and Program*. Urbana, Ill.: National Council of Teachers of English, 1970.

Graves, D. "A New Look at Writing Research." In S. Haley-James (ed.), *Perspectives on Writing in Grades 1–8*. Urbana, Ill.: National Council of Teachers of English, 1981.

Harman, D. *Illiteracy: A National Dilemma*. New York: Cambridge Book Company, 1987.

Harste, J. C., Woodward, V. A., and Burke, C. L. *Language Stories and Literacy Lessons*. Portsmouth, N. H.: Heinemann Educational Books, 1984.

Hunter, C.S.J. "Literacy/Illiteracy in an International Perspective." *World Education Reports*, Spring 1987, pp. 4–7.

Jurmo, P. J. "Learner Participation Practices in Adult Literacy Efforts in the United States." Unpublished Ed.D. dissertation, University of Massachusetts, Amherst, 1987.

Kindervatter, S. *Nonformal Education as an Empowering Process*. Amherst: Center for International Education, University of Massachusetts, 1979.

Kinsey, D. *Evaluation in Nonformal Education*. Amherst: Center for International Education, University of Massachusetts, 1978.

Knowles, M. *Self-Directed Learning*. Chicago: Follett, 1975.

Lerche, R. *Effective Adult Literacy Programs: A Practitioner's Guide*. New York: Cambridge Book Company, 1985.

Mayer, S. *Guidelines for Effective Adult Literacy Programs*. Minneapolis: B. Dalton, 1984.

Rogers, C. R. *Freedom to Learn*. Columbus, Ohio: Merrill, 1969.

Shor, I. *Critical Teaching and Everyday Life*. Boston: South End Press, 1980.

Smith, F. *Understanding Reading*. New York: Holt, Rinehart & Winston, 1978.

Sticht, T. G. *Functional Context Education Workshop Resource Notebook*. San Diego, Calif.: Applied Behavioral & Cognitive Science, 1987.

Watson, D. "The Reader-Thinker's Comprehension-Centered Reading Program." In C. Pennock (ed.), *Reading Comprehension at Four Linguistic Levels*. Newark, Del.: International Reading Association, 1979.

*Paul Jurmo is senior program associate at the Business Council for Effective Literacy in New York City.*

*In participatory literacy programs, learners take active roles in planning, evaluating, and implementing a wide range of instructional activities. They also participate in program governance, student and staff recruitment, public awareness and advocacy, income-generating activities, peer support, and other management-related functions.*

# Instruction and Management: Where Participatory Theory Is Put into Practice

## Paul Jurmo

The preceding chapter presented arguments for why it is important for learners to have active roles in both the instructional and the management components of literacy programs. However, for many interested in developing a learner-centered approach in their programs, the question remains: What specific activities can be used to provide learners with the opportunity to achieve high levels of participation in the program? Or, more simply, what does participatory practice look like? This chapter summarizes the learner-centered activities currently used in the adult literacy field in the United States. For details about the practices, the reader can consult Chapters Three and Four of Jurmo (1987).

### Participatory Practices in Instruction

Traditionally, literacy students have been handed a prescribed set of topics, materials, and activities that they are expected to master. Learner-centered programs give learners some control in the planning of instructional activities. At minimum, learners select from among topics, materials, and activities that others have developed. In the most active cases,

A. Fingeret and P. Jurmo (eds.). *Participatory Literacy Education.*
New Directions for Continuing Education, no. 42. San Francisco: Jossey-Bass, Summer 1989.

learners develop topics, materials, and activities on their own or in collaboration with others.

For example, some programs encourage learners to respond as a group to open-ended questions (such as, "If you could write to any international leader, who would it be and what would you say?"; "Where did you grow up?"). These discussions are then used to help the learners express issues that are on their minds or uses of language with which they need help. The instructor notes these themes and language areas as they emerge in the discussion or tape-records the discussion for later analysis. In this way, learners contribute actively to the process of identifying curriculum topic areas.

In other cases, learners are asked to analyze what they have already achieved in their jobs, in their family lives, in their hobbies, and in other aspects of their lives. By discussing areas in which the learners have developed skills and, in particular, areas in which they use language, instructors help learners to identify the skills and background knowledge that they already possess and bring to the program. These assets are then used as foundation stones for further learning activities.

Learners are also being given the opportunity to participate actively in the evaluation of instructional activities. Many programs encourage learners to give informal feedback to staff on activities as they occur. But formalized mechanisms have also been established. For example, learners hold regular mutual-feedback sessions with their instructors, program supervisors, and fellow learners. They also participate in regular record-keeping procedures in which they not only record their attendance and what they did in a session but assess their own performance and that of their instructors and the materials used.

Learners not only can plan and evaluate what they learn, they can also take active roles in the implementation of instructional activities. In some participatory programs, learners serve as peer teachers of fellow learners who have either the same or a lower skill level. In the first case, learners who have successfully passed through a program or who at least have reached a higher skill level within the program serve as instructors to other learners in the same program or in another program. In the second case, learners work in teams to give feedback and guidance to each other around their performance in instructional activities.

In other situations, learners provide instructional help to individuals who are not participants in adult literacy programs. In an increasingly common use of this idea, adult learners are given guidance in helping their children or grandchildren to deal with literacy-related tasks under the auspices of intergenerational or family reading programs.

Writing is also seen as an area of instruction particularly suited to development of active thinking and self-expression among students. Learner-centered programs have made special use of the word processing and data base capacities of the computer to provide learners with opportunities to write texts around personally meaningful themes. The program newsletter allows learners to practice their writing and self-expression skills in poems, letters to the editor, essays, and stories. And learners write letters to pen pals (for example, learners in other literacy programs or college student volunteers), to program staff and board members, to the news media, or to potential and actual funding sources. Some programs organize writers' workshops to encourage learners to review each others' work, make suggestions, raise questions, and generally pool knowledge while developing individual self-confidence and cooperative behavior. Writing awards given in recognition of specific writing achievements are a mechanism for encouraging learners to write with a clear purpose in mind.

As an alternative to forcing learners to read texts that have limited meaning for themselves and as a way of encouraging learners to reinforce each other's interpretative abilities, some programs have established participatory reading activities. In these activities, learners explore, analyze, and seek help with their reading in the natural ways described by whole-language advocates. In one form of participatory reading, students meet in groups to select and discuss texts that they read in common.

Programs are experimenting with a number of activities that are not usually considered to be instructional in nature. For example, field trips to plays, theaters, television studios, poetry readings, museums, art galleries, and historical sites provide a number of possible benefits: exposure to new areas of knowledge, team building among participants, and awareness that learning can go on outside the classroom. In addition, artistic activities contain many elements of the writing process, including conceptualizing and transforming an idea into a form that others can understand. Examples include role playing, video and photo presentations, and drawing. And learners are now participating in a variety of community development activities that have the dual aims of improving the community and enhancing learners' knowledge of community issues, self-confidence, and abilities to work as part of a team toward a common goal. Examples include voter registration drives and organizing around community issues.

### Participatory Practices in Management

In addition to taking the kinds of active roles in literacy instruction just outlined, learners are taking increased responsibility for various aspects of the management of their programs. For example, learners participate in program governance by serving on program boards of directors or on student advisory councils. Learners on boards of directors are either elected by fellow students or appointed by other board members. In student councils, learners give feedback to program staff about particular student concerns.

· Learners are taking on new roles as paid or volunteer staff within literacy programs. Most commonly they work as staff in the programs in which they have participated as students, but in some cases they move on to work in other programs. Their roles as staff members range from daycare worker for the children of other learners to clerical worker, assistant teacher, or manager of a learning center operated by a larger literacy program. In a few cases, graduates of literacy programs have gone on to found their own neighborhood learning centers.

Learners help some programs to recruit, select, and train staff. For example, learners recruit volunteer tutors by appearing in public service announcements and media interviews and by making tutor recruitment presentations to audiences of community groups, corporate employees, and other sources of volunteers. In some cases, learners also advise staff on the suitability of newly recruited volunteer and paid staff. And learners contribute to the training of newly selected staff members by making presentations, joining in discussions, and participating in role plays during staff training workshops.

Learners are themselves possibly the most effective recruiters of new students for literacy programs. Recognizing this, programs have created roles for current students as well as for graduates in which they help to recruit and orient new participants. For example, learners informally serve as recruiters of new students by telling friends, relatives, and neighbors about the program. The community observes the changes in learners and realizes the positive potential of the program. Learners also take on more formalized roles as recruiters by participating in public service announcements, media interviews, and presentations to community groups. Some groups have arranged for learners to go door to door or to hand out flyers.

Veteran learners commonly make new learners feel comfortable when the newcomers arrive in the program. Building on this natural relationship between veterans and newcomers, programs have asked experienced students to take on formalized roles in assisting with intake of new recruits. To do so, programs have set up student orientation meetings and open houses. Veteran learners are prepared ahead of time about how they can explain the program to newcomers and help newcomers to identify the goals and abilities they bring to the program.

The 1980s saw a major push to increase public awareness of the literacy problem. Coupled with these awareness projects were efforts to increase material support for literacy programs from public-sector funders. Learners have played important roles in public awareness and advocacy activities. For example, learners have appeared in various forms of media coverage—public service announcements, news stories—in which they typically describe their lives before and after they participated in a literacy program. Learners have also taken public speaking engagements on behalf of the literacy field.

In addition to contributing to general public awareness of literacy efforts, learners have served as advocates or lobbyists for the literacy field. In these roles, they concentrate on generating material resources from public sources. Learners speak and write letters to city councils and state legislatures, and they appear at federal hearings. Learners take on these advocacy roles as individuals, as teams of students within programs, and as members of city- and statewide literacy coalitions.

Learners also help to raise funds from private- and public-sector sources in other ways. These funds normally go to support the program, but in some cases they provide income for learners. To raise funds for their programs, learners accompany program staff when they make the rounds of funding sources. It is felt that successful learners are particularly convincing spokespersons for a program. Some programs include examples of student writing in fund-raising packets or encourage learners to serve on the program fund-raising committee. Students on one such committee came up with the idea of asking their employers to make tuition payments to the program, in keeping with the common practice of employer-paid tuition assistance.

Learners have organized book sales, bake sales, raffles, and group outings to raise funds for their programs. And some programs ask learners to make a small weekly tuition payment, both to generate income for the program and to encourage a sense of ownership in the program among learners.

To generate income for learners themselves, programs have created jobs for learners as managers of a program snack bar and as members of a sewing cooperative.

Through participation in such support activities as support groups, recognition events, and social activities, learners are bolstering each other's morale, self-esteem, group identity, and cooperative spirit. These activities also seek to achieve such technical goals as improved communication among program participants, an increased sense of ownership for the program among participants, reduced dropout rates, and increased public awareness of what goes on in the program.

Participation in conferences has historically been something that staff members—not students—do. This situation has changed in recent years as learners themselves have participated in conferences in active ways. Students now observe presentations made by others, make presentations of their own, work in support groups to make recommendations around special student issues, and even plan and organize conferences.

## Conclusion

It is relatively easy to generate lists of participatory literacy education activities. It is far more challenging to incorporate these activities into the daily life of a program. Most educators and learners have no training or experience in sharing the power in instruction or program management and no models to follow. In the next four chapters, the authors share their experiences in taking such activities from the realm of ideas into practice. Recognizing the difficulty of making the transition from traditional to participatory practices, they explain not only the practices that they use but the steps that they took to introduce them into their respective programs.

## Reference

Jurmo, P. J. "Learner Participation Practices in Adult Literacy Efforts in the United States." Unpublished Ed.D. dissertation, University of Massachusetts, Amherst, 1987.

*Paul Jurmo is senior program associate at the Business Council for Effective Literacy in New York City.*

*Contrary to melting pot theories, we have sought self-determination.*

# Community-Based Literacy Educators: Experts and Catalysts for Change

*Raúl Lorenzo Añorve*

I began practicing Freire's (1970, 1973) theory of education during the 1970s because the public school system in this country does not prepare us to become full human beings. As a language teacher, I had been trained to teach specific grammatical objectives based on curricula developed by experts using ready-made texts who did not take into account the learners' sociolinguistic speech and their accumulated knowledge. I had been trained to be skillful at manipulating students so that they would repeat, choose, transfer, and regurgitate information.

Even if I felt privileged to have been admitted to college and proud that I was one of the few Mexicans—the first in my family and my barrio—to have finished, I knew that whatever I was learning was neither relevant to my community nor empowering for my people. When I look back at my high school years and compare my own educational background with today's education in the barrio, I see few changes. Almost 50 percent of the high school students of Mexican descent are still dropping out, only one-fourth of those who graduate get into college, only one-eighth finish college, and only 1 percent of these go to graduate school. I am one of the 1 percent.

A. Fingeret and P. Jurmo (eds.). *Participatory Literacy Education.*
New Directions for Continuing Education, no. 42. San Francisco: Jossey-Bass, Summer 1989.

I finished because of my family's love and because of the drive that I had within me to prove to Ms. Greenish, my high school counselor, and others like her that I could make it through college. I made it despite her advice that I was not college material, despite the three wasted years of drafting, wood shop, and auto shop for which she registered me, and despite the thousands of requests that I received from the local I WANT YOU recruiter.

By reflecting on this experience, I am reaffirming the premise that, since the traditional educational system has not and will not educate Third World and low-income people, it is up to us to educate ourselves and our children. My constant interaction with other "underprivileged" individuals and with their historical and actual struggle gives me a unique opportunity to continue this process of education for liberation.

With long hours of work, I have now helped to organize community-based educational programs in various communities, mainly in the Los Angeles–San Gabriel, California area. Issues affecting participants in a collective teaching and learning environment, such as housing shortages, immigration, welfare rights, education, and decent employment, provide the curricula in community-based education. Participants analyze these themes and are actively involved in solving related problems. This approach to education for liberation or popular education, as it has evolved from its roots in Latin America, differs from traditional formal education not only because it commonly takes place outside a classroom but because it is based on themes generated by the participants themselves and because it uses participatory techniques aimed at getting learners to examine how knowledge is developed and transmitted. In other words, participants reflect on the various activities in which we participate as a community. All this is done from a political perspective.

Education for liberation explicitly enables learners to analyze the texts and the contexts that they encounter so they can transform the oppressive forces that have historically left them on the periphery. However, education for liberation cannot be reduced to form and content. A method based on a dialectical process of interaction between form and content, it aims at reaching a level of action-reflection-action. It is precisely this process that leads community-based groups to the level of consciousness at which participants can analyze the historical and structural causes that shape their reality and take action aimed at overcoming oppressive forces.

I have participated in this type of education for many years. I have lived through exciting struggles that have changed the lives of many and that have changed some policies at the city level. I know that such change is not enough. It will never be enough as long as people lack adequate shelter, adequate food, and decent wages. But at least it is an attempt to work with other human beings less privileged than myself and to acknowledge their contributions to this culture in the process.

Notwithstanding continuous racial tensions, bureaucratic manipulation by public officials, and long meetings, I have seen some participants succeed in forcing city hall to publish public notices in Spanish. Some participants have succeeded in resisting landowners and developers and in maintaining their housing zone as residential. Others have succeeded in having affordable housing in a disputed "blighted" area.

By working with high school Latinos, I have experienced the most wonderful changes that come when teenagers begin to understand how the public school system has failed them, to recognize both blatant and insidious racism, and to struggle to overcome their oppression. Many of the young people with whom I have worked as a community-based instructor at Blair High School in the city of Pasadena have become part of a cadre of facilitators who continue to practice this type of education.

Patricia Guzman is one of the facilitators who was involved in the student walkout of 1981–82 at Blair High School. The students at that time responded to racism by organizing and demanding the continuation of the only class that had been successful in helping them to pass the one hundred fifty-word high school composition requirement. When asked how the class helped her, Patricia replied, "The class taught us how to think critically. I remember that we were asked about things we said, and the teacher wrote them down . . . and he would make us think. The program helped me as a person because we were appreciated not just because he wanted us to pass the class but as people, as individuals. That made me feel good, like a person . . . and it even helped me get into college . . . and it also helped my brother, my friend, and almost all the students get in too. And now I feel sad because I see many high school kids doing nothing, and I think, I wish there was another similar class. It is a shame no one is out there helping."

Another young Latina who like Patricia has not left her community and who is part of the struggle to change the present oppressive system is Matilde Soria. An undergraduate student at U.C.L.A., Matilde coordinates a student volunteer educational program sponsored by U.C.L.A. She has been instrumental in securing resources from U.C.L.A. to be used by community people who otherwise would not be able to afford it. She, along with other student volunteers, has forged a direct link between the Latino community in Pasadena and U.C.L.A. In this way, information about needs, recruitment, requirements, and other important information is communicated accurately.

Matilde is active in the cultural, historical, and political events that take place at U.C.L.A. These include the Cinco de Mayo celebration, South Africa Solidarity Day, and demonstrations to eliminate institutional racism and improve minority recruitment. Matilde transports community members to the U.C.L.A. campus in order to enable them to participate. In other words, their tax dollars are no longer wasted.

Jose Robles, a former adult learner and a laborer, volunteers his time at a community-based school after he has worked eight to ten hours of manual labor. It is rewarding to work with people like Jose who believe in respecting their co-learners and in humanizing the process of education in a community-based organization. Jose explains how learners are involved in the program in which he volunteers. "Those who are just a little bit more advanced teach. For example, I am one of them. I started as a student, and now I teach, and I like it. We have had others like, for example, Marta, Agustin, Maria Pacheco . . . and another named Maria . . . and we motivate them so they can continue. And I think this system is a good one, because I know that as an adult I have a better idea how I learned. And thus I can explain to them in a very simple way how I learned. Because the student knows just a little bit less than I do."

**Workplace/Work Force Literacy**

The participatory methods to which Jose alludes are essential in developing literacy programs for the workplace. I began developing educational programs for private industry in the early 1980s before workplace literacy programs came into vogue. Lack of communication between immigrant workers and Anglo managers was the overriding reason why companies decided to hire me to develop a language program. What I proposed to them then and what I continue to use today is what I call the *learner-centered approach*. I use this term and not *liberatory education* for obvious reasons. I make it clear that a learner-centered approach is based on the knowledge that the participants already possess and that it is independent of the setting. After I introduce the concept, managers often begin to recognize how much of their workers' knowledge is untapped. Managers certainly are interested in an instructional method that will enhance worker productivity. A cost-effective program sells.

Because of tremendous competition from Japan and Western Europe, many U.S. companies have been driven to adopt high-tech production methods. How to train a functionally illiterate work force has become a popular question for academic researchers, and for managers it is a continuing challenge. For me, it has created a space in which I can implement a more humane approach to literacy education.

In a participatory approach, workers strengthen their oral, reading, writing, analytical, and teamwork skills through active study of issues of direct concern to them. They analyze issues of discrimination, labor laws, wages and salaries, union contracts, maternity leave, promotion, and so forth.

In the initial assessment phase of program development, I tour the plant, taking photographs of worksites, machines, and so on. I interview supervisors and managers, helping them to understand the program while asking them to identify areas of concern for employee basic skills. For example, I may ask how they would train a new worker and what skills they would focus on. I look at the company's training facilities. I ask how they communicate with workers. I also study the production process so I can understand the context in which the learners work. Along the way, I collect sample reading and writing materials, which can include union contracts, posters, and other "codes" representing workplace themes.

In the next step of the assessment phase, I meet with the workers in two-hour sessions. I show them enlargements of the photos I took and ask them to identify what they see. In this discussion process, key themes and vocabulary emerge for treatment later in classes.

By interviewing both management and workers, I seek to clarify the relationship between workers' knowledge and management's assumptions. I do not focus initially on identifying skill gaps (that is, on workers' "deficits"). Instead, I try to pull out what workers already know. In the process, the workers' self-esteem is reinforced. Traditional skills assessments tend to focus on deficits, and they are therefore intimidating to workers. Workers typically have had bad experiences with tests in school, and they often suspect that workplace testing will be used to limit their opportunities for advancement. I do conduct testing, but only if the workers themselves ask for it. To ensure confidentiality, test results are shared only with the learner involved.

When classes get under way, a typical small group has learners reviewing the photos, identifying problems that they encounter in a situation, and analyzing those problems. Key words and phrases used in these discussions are recorded. The language used in these sessions varies with the workers' fluency in English. Technical English-language terms commonly found and used in the plant are given special emphasis to ensure that workers understand them. This emphasis not only helps the workers but responds to the company's interest in improving worker productivity and communication skills.

In this process, sensitive issues (for example, racism, sexism) inevitably arise. I tell this to management up front and explain that both technical and social issues have to be dealt with directly if the company really wants to have a work force with critical thinking skills. I also explain that discussing such issues can help to clear the air at a worksite because it allows workers to vent concerns and iron out differences that hurt employee morale. Unions usually support such an approach, and I have not yet encountered management that did not support the approach when its members had had a chance to think about it. Workers at one company wrote a letter to the chief executive officer requesting that the class be continued. After reviewing the sometimes sensitive issues that workers were discussing, he agreed to continue the class.

Evaluation activities take several forms. For example, I look at how well workers have improved their ability to read, write, and speak. I do this periodically by giving informal tests focused on grammar, vowel sounds, or ability to respond to technical uses of English. For example, I ask in English, "Where is the fire alarm?" Or I ask them to write a memo. Because workers themselves have asked for job-specific tests, I develop such tests for each worker. The tests give workers a sense of their relative progress. The results are recorded in a notebook for each worker, because workers identify "having a book" as a sign that they are really receiving an education.

As part of the evaluation, I interview supervisors. I ask whether they have noticed any progress in participating workers. I ask the supervisors whether they have heard workers talking about the class and, if so, what the workers have said.

I summarize my findings in a written report, attaching samples of materials written by workers themselves. This approach to evaluation attempts to provide data that are of concrete use to all concerned: workers, unions, management, and educators.

## Key Issues

A fundamental question for me is how to empower workers and at the same time maintain a program that ensures adequate access to opportunities for promotion, adequate wages, and sick leave and maternity leave while improving workers' skills.

I am concerned that workplace literacy programs will be used to admit a few and eliminate many. Managers will use testing for high-tech positions to justify getting rid of employees with low reading skills, and those who do qualify will have to perform additional tasks. Worst of all, more demanding communications skills criteria will be used to discriminate against those who have an accent. The potential for misusing the literacy program by managers is real. I share the following comment made by a participant in one of our workplace programs to remind myself of workers caught in their future without being consulted: "Look at my hands! See them? These hands have contributed to the wealth of this company, and not once in twenty years have I had to read English, nor have I had to speak it in order to do my work. Now they're telling me that I need to read English in order to do the same work and compete with another worker?"

## Conclusion

Community-based educators must be prepared to deal effectively with the key issues just raised. To do so, we must take an active role in workplace literacy efforts. We must be willing to create a space for ourselves in workplace programs, as we have historically done in our communities where—contrary to melting pot theories—we have sought self-determination for neglected people.

Businesses and public policy makers should recognize that community-based educators have the expertise needed to develop educational programs capable of developing the skilled work force that the economy needs. It remains to be seen how the U.S. government and private industry will respond to the problem of workplace literacy. The existing position papers indicate a growing sense of urgency about work force basic skills. But those in power have shown little interest in considering community-based analysis of the causes and solutions for workplace illiteracy. Instead, those who control policy and funding have basically tried to maintain the status quo vis-à-vis work force education.

As for me, I will continue to ask the same questions of managers and others: What are the causes of illiteracy? How do workers learn a task? What training is provided? What types of manuals exist? And how does literacy fit in?

As community-based educators, we must continue to assert ourselves as experts in this field. We must network and share our experiences. We must synthesize these experiences and act socially and politically to create a strong community-based educational alternative.

I raise these and other, similar questions because my own experience shows that few opportunities for good education are given to people of color and other low-income people. I want those in control to know that learner-centered education programs offer an important solution—perhaps the only humane solution—to the economic and social problems facing us as a nation.

We all need to remember: Illiteracy is not a choice. No one chooses to live in a poverty-stricken area earning minimum wages for ten, fifteen, or twenty years. There are plenty of resources available for training, education, and an overall equitable distribution of wealth.

**References**

Freire, P. *Pedagogía del oprimido* (The pedagogy of oppression). Mexico: Siglo XXI, 1970.
Freire, P. *Education for Critical Consciousness*. New York: Seabury Press, 1973.

*Raúl Lorenzo Añorve is a community-based literacy coordinator for California Literacy, Inc., and codirector of La Escuela de la Comunidad in Pasadena, California.*

*Each person is literally bringing a life to the group.*

# Partnership for Change

*Marilyn A. Boutwell*

The term *partnership learning* often creates more confusion than understanding, raising such questions as "Does that mean we're equals?" "Who's in control?" "Do we withhold what we know?" "Why don't you teach me?" These reactions reveal the depth of mistrust and fear of the power that we have as learners. Somewhere along the line, many people lose a basic belief in themselves—that they can and must be active in their own learning process.

Two-year-olds know better. They believe that they are the center of the universe, and they initiate and actively pursue every opportunity to experiment with boundaries, possibilities, and methods of communication in order to exert some control over their relationship to the environment. Too often, this energy is dissipated or destroyed.

Learning partnerships require respect, open communication, and a sense of mutual responsibility. In such relationships, language is a social act and a catalyst for change. Change can be both confrontational and threatening. One of the most confrontational situations that I have experienced began in 1969 when I tried to "teach" at a state hospital for emotionally disturbed children and adolescents. They refused to be "taught." We had to find some common ground, or we would have had no future together. They gave me a gift, for I had to learn the importance and dimensions of listening. This has served me well in every classroom in which I have worked since—whether in rural or urban schools, on

A. Fingeret and P. Jurmo (eds.). *Participatory Literacy Education.*
New Directions for Continuing Education, no. 42. San Francisco: Jossey-Bass, Summer 1989.

Native American reservations, on college campuses, in teachers' lunchrooms, or in community settings. Learning communities require collaboration among all participants to create a safe, respectful environment in which each individual can be and is heard.

I am reminded of a passage in an essay by Ursula K. LeGuin (1985, pp. 116-117): "One by one we live, soul by soul. The person, single person. Community is the best we can hope for, and community for most people means touch. We can form a circle, but we cannot be the circle. The circle, the true society, is formed of single bodies and single souls. If not, it is not formed at all."

In 1983, several staff members of Literacy Volunteers of New York City (LVNYC) attended a course on writing that I taught at the Teachers College, Columbia University Summer Writing Institute. Later they hired me to form writing workshop groups for adult beginning readers in their program. As I began at their corporate sites, I was astonished by how adamant the adult learners were about their belief that they had failed as learners. Although the sites were full of student-tutor pairs, the students would not relinquish their feelings of isolation. They not only could not see that others shared similar feelings, but many felt that their learning would cease if their own tutor left.

I worked with students, tutors, and staff to form writing groups that met on a regular basis to write about things that students cared about and to share individual writings with the aim of getting responses that would help them to substantiate or clarify their meaning. Occasionally, the groups held sitewide celebrations to read their works. Sites began to buzz with an energy for sharing learning and with an appreciation of commonalities as well as differences.

**The Intensive Program**

This energy did not automatically extend to reading, so the next year I piloted an intensive reading and writing program. Eight tutors worked for three evenings exploring their own learning process. Then they split into cotutoring pairs to form four learning groups with six adult new readers in each.

The students resisted. They were reluctant to give up their individual tutors. For example, Emily, an adult learner, recalls, "When I first came to this program, I didn't think I'd get anything out of it. I was doing good with a proper tutor on a one-to-one. So I worried. . . . I was in a shell. I didn't talk. My daughter said the other day when I was talking to my grandson, 'Mom, you're talking so much now, it's wonderful.' And I didn't even know I was. I think reading and writing and talking about it here did that for me."

I learned a great deal from the adult learners that year about shells, walls of silence, poison building up inside now spilling out, and hope.

The more they acknowledged themselves as learners, the more they read, wrote, and shared their struggles. Adrian passed a citywide painter's test that he had failed three times. Calvin chose to read books about Native Americans, admitting it was "a little sentimental thing there because I'm partially Indian." Rosa became closer to her daughter, who now "comes to our celebrations to hear me read my stories. Sometimes I even read and talk to her, ask her opinions."

One-to-one instruction often becomes another form of isolation and dependence. In small-group instruction, students are encouraged to respect their own knowledge and experience and that of others and to work together to become independent, competent learners. Tutors, who act as facilitators, must learn to be keen observers and active listeners. They facilitate learning by modeling techniques, bringing individual and group strengths to the forefront, and utilizing teaching moments as they arise within the context of the students' work.

For these reasons, the cotutors of each learning group encouraged students to choose individual reading material that reflected their interests and to write about things that were meaningful to them. The time was divided between actual reading and writing tasks and time spent together to share their work and discoveries. Students were encouraged to concentrate on composing meaning. Spelling, new vocabulary, and skill work occurred after the composing processes had been completed, and they were taught in the context of the students' own work.

Tutors who were comfortable with reflecting upon their learning during the year expressed enthusiasm about experimenting with script writing, drama, poetry, and fiction. They encouraged their readers and writers to collaborate in similar ways. Margarette says of her experiences that, "The first thing was to help my group realize they had something in common—they were all learning to read and write. When they realized that, they found out how they could help each other. There was a catharsis in that. They could begin to develop their own self-confidence, share and rely on one another as well as on us. They became bolder in everything they did."

But this style of work was not comfortable for other tutors. For example, Liz says that her experience "wasn't so good. I found little things did work, but I didn't keep track. I confused the students more than anything else. Once I realized that, I'd already dug myself in this hole, and I couldn't seem to get out of it."

In the fall of 1985, Eli Zal, the new executive director of LVNYC, asked me to become full-time associate director. His enthusiasm for student involvement in learning coincided with mine. Ellen Steiner, a tutor from the intensive program, replaced me as its coordinator. We decided to use the intensive program as a teaching model to help other tutors and students from other LVNYC sites to begin their own learning groups.

Ellen entered the position with these reflections: "One thing I want to remember that I learned last year is that every adult has something important to say, and each person is literally bringing a life to the group. The relationship between students and tutors is reciprocal. It's not passive. The interaction is concentrated on creation rather than remediation. I find little neutral territory in what people want to read and write."

During the next year, my hope that the intensive program could serve as a model for instruction was shaken. My hope was based on a false premise—that the program would remain unchanged. Instead, it went through stages of turmoil and redefinition. During one such period, Ellen said to me, "The students say they're bored. Some don't even come anymore. The tutors are upset. Some are so frustrated they're going back to a directive approach. I don't know what's going on."

It took us a while to remember the importance of active listening. We interviewed the students and discovered that the term *boring* came with many underlying positives. For example, Forrestine was no longer content to confine herself to autobiographical pieces. She wanted to write scathing letters to Mayor Koch demanding his respect for the homeless people huddled in her subway stop. Wilson wanted to transfer to "a full-time program where I can learn a trade." Emily wanted to learn how to organize a neighborhood petition to a local grocery store that "sold goods that are out of date and no good anymore." Calvin questioned everybody's opinion, and his group became a battleground of dissent.

The more we heard, the more we understood that the program had not grown with its students. In group meetings, complaints were aired, and new goals were defined. Several groups began to study their own group process in order to teach groups at other sites. One group studied critical thinking and the power behind the question, Why? Some students became involved in providing orientation for new students. Others helped with training sessions for new students. The potential for leadership grew.

## Students on Staff

As adult learners gained confidence and began to speak to their needs, I gained insight into my own role. In fall 1985, Eli and I decided to hire an LVNYC student to provide us with insight and guidance on student needs. Ralph Arrindell was hired as student advocate. He continued as a student, but he provided full-time advice to staff. He enrolled in our twenty-four-hour tutor-training program and answered all incoming calls from potential students. His own experience as a new reader and writer helped to ease new students' fears. But his inability to fill out student file cards gave us a glimpse of issues that we would have to face on how to bridge the gap between knowledge and written language skills.

Eli began to take Ralph to corporate meetings and fund raisers. The first time, Ralph stood and simply spoke his name. He admitted, "I couldn't find the rest of my words." But by the end of the first year, Ralph became a principal speaker at corporate fund raisers, workshops, tutor trainings, and in the news media.

Ralph and I met weekly. He explained the emotional barriers that confronted his own sense of being an effective learner. I showed him ways of transforming his journal writings about his learning process into professional articles and speeches. Our partnership extended to conferences where we often shared our give-and-take relationship with other teachers and students.

The next year, Ralph formed a student committee comprised of two adult learners from each LVNYC site. They were to meet monthly to discuss student needs. Ralph worked with the committee its first year, but the working relationship was fraught with conflict. Ralph's own skills and experience had expanded. He often became impatient with other adults who were reluctant to trust advice based on his new knowledge and enthusiasm for involvement. This eventually led to a separation between the paid advocacy staff and the student committee. The advocacy team now consisted not only of Ralph and a staff support person but of two more paid student advocates—Forrestine Bragg and Calvin Miles.

The separation was perhaps a necessary one. Both the student committee and the advocacy component needed to answer these questions for themselves: What are the roles, responsibilities, and relationships between staff and student leaders? No one really knew, because this was new territory. Calvin described the conflict in these terms: "I was excited when my own peers elected me. I thought I would represent the site and meet with a larger group to discuss issues. The first few meetings were okay, but then they became students knocking each other out over Ralph's supervisor. . . . I felt she was there to keep us organized. They saw her as a threat. I backed out of the committee. I felt like we'd be arguing all the time. By arguing, I mean that my views differed from theirs—staff separate versus staff as helpers."

This type of conflict over working roles extended into the relationship between the advocates and their staff supervisor. During the first two years, five different staff members had provided support at different times. The kind of support that they gave depended greatly upon the individual. This led to inconsistencies and to changing expectations.

Although misunderstandings and changes in working relationships occurred, the actual curricula of the advocacy component became both clearer and expanded. Educational modules on such issues as black history, voter registration and education, and accuracy in information on AIDS were created in response to students' actual needs and interests, and Students & Teachers in Partnership cosponsored a citywide conference with Lehman College. The team also initiated peer tutoring groups and explored new avenues of communication that led to changes in LVNYC policies and procedures.

## A Student on the Board of Directors

The board of directors was one avenue of communication that had not been utilized. Although a board position for a student existed, no student occupied it prior to 1986. When the student committee was created, the understanding was that peers would elect one member to serve on the board.

Inez Seda, the first student to serve on the board, remembers, "Before I'd go to a board meeting, I'd talk to Eli. . . . He'd tell me what to expect, go over the paperwork, and explain a lot of things. Then we'd try to figure out what I'd talk about. . . . We were both in the dark. . . . When I went for the first time, it was like breaking ground. The people were nice. They would call every meeting to order, and they would talk about everything they had to say. Sometimes what I was going to say, Eli had already said some of it by the time they got to me. After a while, it became boring. I didn't think I was serving a purpose."

Once again, the term *boring* indicated an unmet need—how to create a meaningful partnership between the board and the student body.

## The Student Committee

Crucial to the student-board partnership was the strengthening of the student committee itself. When Ralph first went from site to site encouraging students to run for election, it became clear no one really knew what the committee might be. Pearlie Walters recalls her first election in these words: "Ralph came to my site and asked me to run. Clifton, a brand-new student, said he would run. He didn't know what he was getting into. I said, 'All right, I'll run, too.' We were supposed to give speeches. I never even thought about the speech, because I had no intention of being student representative. Clifton gave his speech. Then I was to do mine. I'm standing there trying to talk my way out of being representative. I said I thought Clifton would be very good and that everybody should vote for him. All the students sat there so patient waiting on me to finish. Then Ralph says, 'Pearlie, we need two representatives from this site.' I said, 'Oh, well, what the hell. I'll do the best I can.' "

The student committee had a difficult time defining its agenda and role. By December, frustration turned into anger. As Pearlie remembers it, "Each person said what they felt about the meeting, the organization, and everything. One student said he was wasting his time here. It was a hot meeting . . . I walked to the subway with Ralph that night. He was saying, 'It's not supposed to be like this.' I said, 'Ralph, you have no control over what happens. People said exactly what was on their minds. That's good that it came out.' Eli came to see me later on. He was concerned about all the anger. I told him the same as I told Ralph."

The committee's first project was to sponsor a programwide party. They successfully organized and held the party in December. It has since become an annual event. Their next project was to sell candy to earn money to send students to a national literacy conference. Just prior to that project, the committee had severed its direct ties with Ralph's supervisor, who had been liaison to their committee. Pearlie describes this separation as role conflict: "I met with Ralph's supervisor and said, 'On our meeting tapes, we hear nobody's voice but yours and just two students. You don't give the rest of us a chance to speak. Not that we don't want you here, but we need somebody to take notes. If you take notes, then fine, you can stay.' She got all upset and said that wasn't what she was there for. She left."

So the committee, under the unofficial direction of Pearlie, undertook the fund raiser themselves. Pearlie describes the difficulties within the committee: "I wanted to get the whole committee organized. I wanted a chairperson, secretary, treasurer, the whole works. One student didn't want it. She said, 'Who are you going to get to volunteer their time?' She pushed it down so much, nobody went for it."

Pearlie took charge. Through all the difficulties that ensued, the committee worked together to net over $1,400 from the project. Pearlie felt proud of its success but resentful that she had carried the responsibility for its outcome alone. She vowed never to support another fund raiser. But several months later, Ralph approached the committee to sponsor a student dance and fashion show aimed at earning more money to send students to the conference.

Hesitantly, the committee agreed to explore possible dance locations. Pearlie describes what they found as "too small, and most of them were dumps." They then asked Ralph to explore further. He did and found a suitable place that was also expensive. The committee was indecisive despite Ralph's urging. Many expressed fear of spending so much money and possibly going in the hole. Ralph assured them that he'd learned from being on staff that if you put money into doing a fund raiser well, you gained greater returns in the end. Few members believed him.

Ralph took it upon himself to take the risk. He borrowed the money from Eli to finance the deposit, but he did it without the committee's approval. Pearlie expressed the committee's sense of betrayal and anger: "I told Ralph, 'You don't do that, not on the behalf of the student committee without asking them first.' " The student advocates went on to sponsor the dance and fashion show themselves, and Ralph felt that he could no longer work with the committee.

By the summer, the student committee was reduced to five members trying to work alone. Meetings revolved around arguments and complaints. Pearlie had about given up when a new student representative, Creola Kelly, arrived one evening. "Creola asked how we were organized. I said, 'Believe it or not, all we have is this tape recorder.' She said, 'I'm in the wrong place. When the students elected me, I thought I was getting into something. But I'm getting into nothing. I'm out.' I said, 'Don't say that. You are the first person in a long time who came to the committee that wants to help. I think between you and me we're going to get this thing organized. But I need your help—someone to help, rather than fight.' "

This partnership led the committee to define specific roles and functions for the committee. By the fall, they were fully organized with Pearlie as chairperson. They invited me to attend a meeting to define what the organization's expectations were of the committee. As a result, the committee defined its own philosophy and purpose as well as inviting me to become the official note taker for the committee—a role I have occupied ever since.

During 1987 and 1988, the committee sent students to national conferences, advised staff on program policies, defined unmet student needs, and began to hold monthly student meetings at sites. Eli and I hired consultants to give students the support they requested in building leadership skills.

Pearlie's assessment is positive: "We've learned a lot from that, mainly how to communicate. We sit down, and we listen to what each other is saying, rather than just sitting there talking. We have respect for each other. That makes it different . . . I thought they'd be telling us something we should do and shouldn't do. But what they are really doing is getting us to look at ourselves and know what we can do, rather than leave the decisions 'til someone can help. We have all those leadership qualities in ourselves, and we just didn't know it."

**Lessons Learned**

The 1988–89 year was one in which we looked at where we have been and listened to what we all—students, tutors, staff, and board members—have learned. We gave the year to ourselves. It helped us to go through a five-year strategic planning process that required active participation from students, tutors, staff, and board members. We redefined our mission statement, created five-year goals, and set specific objectives that we will review and redefine each year.

In looking back, it seems important that we have our vision of what learning can be up front and clearly defined. Then everyone can enter the process by making informed choices as to what fits for them and what does not. We have discovered that it's not that we all must share a common vision of learning but that we all must see that our own personal vision is compatible.

Creating new avenues for the sharing of ideas and fluid communication are essential to this process. I remember when I first came to LVNYC to set up writing groups. I spent the first several visits sitting down with individual students, tutors, and staff just listening to them before we even began planning groups. The time spent on getting to know one another is essential in creating partnership relationships.

With this in mind, we value any avenue of direct communication. The student committee is now working to form support groups for new students entering the program to help allay fears, clarify what active learning involves, and help new students voice their own goals and expectations. The committee is also working with the advocacy team to make travel plans and run fund-raising events to send fifty students to the next national conference. Several committee members now serve on board working committees.

Tutor support is as crucial as student support. Site coordinators are forming tutor support teams to share and explore their own learning about "teaching." The tutor committee is working with the leadership consultant to define its own roles, responsibilities, and relationships. New models for tutor training include an apprenticeship period of working directly with experienced students and tutors.

We have begun to redesign and institute a student-centered assessment process. The process will help students to learn ways of assessing their own individual progress. A system of program evaluation will be designed to determine clearly where learning is being effected.

Rita Katcher, coordinator of the student advocates, describes her role as one of "learning how to step back and let the students on staff take responsibility for whatever we do. Whatever we do for projects has to be responsive to the issues requested by the student body as a whole. This is a new way of working for me—learning how to let go. It's exciting and frightening at the same time."

We are learning new questions to consider and we are learning about ourselves. Student advocate Calvin Miles explains his challenge as follows: "As students on staff, we were looked upon as having too much strength. We were working too hard and too strong. We made a mistake, too. We didn't stop to see what was behind the anger we felt from students. Maybe students always saw us as a step up. Maybe they felt we were threatening. We have to be conscious of that. I have to be conscious of that even more now, because I've grown since I've been on staff, and I have to step back more. . . . I have to look at my own learning so I can explain it to others and make sense. I need to stay closely involved at sites. . . . If I lose touch with the students, I lose touch with what is real. I see myself as their student."

We are learning how to stay in touch with each other as we come closer as a community of learners. Some of the people who contributed to our understanding were lost in the struggle. Liz did not continue tutoring and left voicing a sense of failure. Ralph left after encountering difficulties on defining roles and responsibilities with his new supervisor. Many others stayed. Without their determination and faith in partnership learning, we would not be where we are now, nor would we be as excited as we are about what we may create in the future together.

## Reference

LeGuin, U. K. *The Language of the Night.* New York: Berkley, 1985.

*Marilyn A. Boutwell is director of education for Literacy Volunteers of New York City and cochairperson of The Coalition of Adult Education Providers in New York City.*

*Participatory approaches to assessment evolve from critical reflection on current practice and raise broad questions about literacy teaching and learning that have implications for many aspects of program development.*

# Learner-Centered Literacy Assessment: An Evolving Process

Susan L. Lytle, Alisa Belzer, Katherine Schultz, Marie Vannozzi

Across the United States, literacy programs for adults differ quite dramatically from one another, yet most have in common a concern with learner assessment over time. Many are required for the purposes of funding or accountability to administer standardized tests, modified or adapted from those designed for children and based on the assumption that literacy is a set of technical skills for which there can be national norms irrespective of variations related to learners' goals, community, and culture. Many programs question the validity or usefulness of these assessments, yet they struggle to identify alternatives more compatible with the purposes of participatory education.

In this chapter, we describe the process of developing a set of learner-centered assessment procedures within a large, urban literacy agency.

The authors have been collaborating on the Adult Literacy Evaluation Project, an action research project funded by the Philadelphia National Bank through the Literacy Research Center, University of Pennsylvania.

A. Fingeret and P. Jurmo (eds.). *Participatory Literacy Education.*
New Directions for Continuing Education, no. 42. San Francisco: Jossey-Bass, Summer 1989.

Through a collaborative action research project involving staff and students from the literacy program with faculty and graduate students from a nearby university, we have explored forms of assessment that reflect a sociocultural view of literacy and learning. We begin by describing some of our assumptions about assessment, literacy, and learning. Next, because we see assessment as deeply contextualized, we characterize the literacy program where the project is ongoing. Then we describe the three phases or stages that have thus far been needed in order to design and begin to use participatory approaches to assessment. Last, from the particulars of our experience, we extrapolate issues and questions that suggest some directions for learner-centered assessment and discuss some of the associated problems and contradictions.

It is important to say at the outset that our notions of learner centeredness have changed considerably during this process and that they are still evolving. We attribute this change to what we now regard as a paradox in our experience—the fact that the impetus for changes in assessment procedures came from some (but not all) program staff and from staff but not explicitly from learners. We wanted to create the conditions that made it possible for learners to participate in assessment, yet needed to learn how to take direction from the adults themselves. We have also come to understand that participatory literacy assessment is often discontinuous with previous experience of learning in school and therefore contrary to the expectations of most adult students and some members of program staff as well. As a result, participatory assessment may be encouraging or empowering for adult learners at the same time that it causes conflict by creating new roles and power relationships for staff and students.

Engaging in the process of developing participatory assessment procedures has meant uncovering previously unexamined and even conflicting ideologies about literacy education. It has also raised fundamental questions about the relationships between participatory assessment and the nature of teaching and learning. By examining critically some of our own attitudes and experiences, we endeavor to show how complex and fragile the process of inventing learner-centered practices may sometimes be.

## Assumptions About Literacy, Assessment, and Learning

Current traditional assessment procedures—by which we mean standardized tests and other outside-in methods that make adults the objects of someone's scrutiny—have two drawbacks: They fail to capture the richness and complexity of adult learning, and they reinforce a view of literacy as a set of autonomous, technical skills divorced from meaningful context. Moreover, the diagnosis of reading ability as grade levels is misleading, and it often confuses and discourages adults, who may drop out of programs because they find the tests embarrassing, stressful, and reminiscent of past failures in school. Assessment, both initial and ongoing, is important to adults themselves who are seeking some assurance that their efforts to learn have been successful. When teachers are testers and the instruments are limited to quantitative descriptions of skills and deficits, the process of assessing learning becomes onerous and self-defeating.

A contrasting framework or perspective is provided by current cross-cultural research on literacy, which sketches a compelling picture of interesting and important differences within and across communities. When literacy is understood as playing many different roles in the lives of individuals and communities, one must further acknowledge that there is a plurality of literacies, culturally organized and learned in specific settings. According to this perspective, individuals and groups vary in their purposes for reading and writing, in the texts that they choose, and in the contexts for performance of reading and writing abilities. Rather than a technical skill or a feature or attribute of a person, literacy becomes a range of practices or activities (Scribner, 1987). Intra- and interindividual differences in literacy reflect the context of use, so that each person's literacy is by definition unique and dynamic (Lytle and Schultz, in press).

Assessing literacy as practice means exploring the particular types of reading and writing that adults regard as meaningful under different circumstances and that reflect their own purposes and aspirations. In the assessment process, adults need to examine their own relation to learning, their uses of literacy to inform and address their own questions and needs. If literacy in a community is indeed organized as collaborative practice, as Reder (1987) has argued, then assessing change over time involves paying attention to what counts as literacy to different groups or individuals within their communities.

A learner-centered or participatory approach to assessment is therefore built on several assumptions, among them that adults come to programs with particular goals, with previous experiences with literacy, and with perceptions of reading, writing, and learning that all affect what and how they learn. Because assessment communicates a view of literacy, making decisions about procedures and relationships is critical to programs that aim for meaningful learner participation. In learner-centered assessment, adults are very actively involved. They structure the process and join with staff and other students to investigate their own literacy practices in ways that link directly to instruction and that may in turn be integrated with instruction.

By translating this sociocultural perspective into assessment procedures and using them over time with adults, we have developed a conceptual framework that in its current form identifies four dimensions of literacy learning: practices, strategies and interests, perceptions, and goals. As Lytle and Schultz (in press) have noted, the first dimension focuses on the role of literacy in everyday life. Learners describe the variety of settings in which they engage in literacy practices, including what, when, where, and with whom they read and write as well as their mode of engagement in literacy activities. Home, community, and work environments are explored in order to understand the social networks and contexts in which learners now use or want to use literacy skills. To assess the adult learner's repertoire of reading and writing strategies and interests, a variety of texts and tasks are used, including an array of materials, such as newspapers, novels, photographs of local street signs, and adult learner-authored texts. Criteria for assessing growth include increasingly efficient and effective use of a range of reading and writing strategies, an increasingly broad range of task-appropriate types of trans-actions with texts, and increased ability to use written language for mul-tiple purposes. The third dimension of the assessment focuses on adult learners' metacognitive perceptions of reading and writing, teaching and learning. This dimension involves exploration of adults' theories of read-ing and writing, including their own learning histories and their current conceptions of reading and writing processes, tasks, texts, and strategies. Finally, adults identify, prioritize, and discuss their goals and purposes for literacy learning based on a list of goals compiled from past adult participants in this literacy program. The four dimensions just described are used to structure assessment. An ongoing portfolio of reading and writing artifacts can function as the primary resource for selecting, ana-lyzing, and synthesizing data to indicate growth. At any point in time, procedures can be used to construct a profile that captures not only the four dimensions but also their interrelationships—a rich and nuanced picture of the literacy beliefs, experiences, and abilities of the adult. Over time, each dimension represents a continuum of literacy development. Figure 1 summarizes these features of learner-centered assessment as they have evolved in our project.

## Context for the Assessment Project

The context in which these participatory approaches to learner assess-ment were developed is a literacy program, the Center for Literacy (CFL), which grew dramatically during the first three years of the project, a fact that both enhanced and complicated our efforts. Pushed by the national literacy campaigns and an active board of corporate, foundation, and educational leaders and supported by a large infusion of state funding, CFL (the largest such program in Philadelphia) grew from 440 students in 1985 to more than 1,600 in 1988. Participants meet at seventy sites located in neighborhoods throughout the city. A critical feature of CFL

**Figure 1. Design for Assessment in the Adult Literacy Evaluation Project (ALEP)**

| Dimension of Assessment Procedures | Purposes: Learner and Program | Processes | Criteria for Assessing Change |
|---|---|---|---|
| Literacy practices: role of literacy/ learning in everyday life | To describe contexts and practices | Discuss uses in home, community, workplace, and so on | Frequency and variety in types of participation in literacy-related events |
| Reading, writing, and learning strategies and interests | To provide an opportunity to display and take risks in displaying reading and writing repertoire | Construct and analyze portfolio of literacy activities; range of reading and writing texts and tasks | More efficient and effective use of a wider range of strategies |
| Perceptions of reading and writing, teaching and learning | To understand adults' histories of reading and writing, teaching and learning; knowledge of processes, strategies, texts, and tasks | Discuss perceptions in general and in relation to specific activities | Changes in knowledge about reading and writing processes, strategies, texts, and tasks |
| Goals | To identify current abilities and interests and set priorities for learning | Discuss and complete check-list of goals (home and family, social and business, personal and job-related) | Demonstration of competence at self-selected tasks related to goals; setting new goals; reassessing previous goals; changing priorities |

Source: Lytle and Schultz, in press.

is its commitment to offering a flexible program that can meet the diverse needs of adult students by offering one-to-one tutoring by volunteers as well as small, staff-taught classes. Increasing the number of classes offered not only meets the need to accommodate increased numbers of students but also reflects the agency's responsiveness to requests from business and industry, social service and educational agencies, and community groups. CFL has recently sought opportunities to begin a neighborhood partnership project aimed at developing educational services related to specific community needs, but for the most part the program can be regarded as individually oriented (Fingeret, 1984) in the sense that tutoring and class sessions are not linked systematically to the particular needs and problems of local neighborhoods.

Much of the work involved in managing this large literacy program is done by a professional staff housed at the program's central offices and by a group of (geographical) area coordinators whose number grew from four to nine so that the number of students could increase. The agency has a somewhat flattened hierarchical structure that makes the director responsible for planning, fund raising, and grant writing (among other things), while a middle management group performs a variety of organizational and supervisory functions. However, the jobs are not so neatly defined, because coordinators sometimes tutor and supervisors have some direct contact with students in a variety of settings. There is no single central meeting place where students gather regularly for instruction or other program functions.

The size of CFL, its complexity as an organization, and its primary orientation toward providing one-to-one literacy services to adult learners seem to be obstacles to participatory education and thus to participatory modes of assessment. Yet, CFL staff, individually and collectively, subscribe to a curriculum that is learner centered, that is, to a curriculum based on an assessment of each student's goals, interests, and needs. CFL has a tradition of innovation and experimentation within the generally mainstream pattern associated with the use of volunteer tutors as teachers. Although few such projects have been produced collaboratively with learners, CFL has over the years produced tutor handbooks and other curricular materials that are based on a nonstandardized, reflective approach to teaching and learning.

It is not surprising then that interest in learner-centered assessment began to surface at CFL. Dissatisfaction with standardized tests led one staff member (Eno, 1985) to criticize CFL's past use of tests and call for change. In fall 1985, interest among faculty and other students at the university in developing alternative forms of assessment was thus matched by the deeply felt need on the part of some CFL staff for a form of assessment that would be more congruent with the intent of the program as a whole. What was not clear initially was the extent to which *learner-centered* at CFL meant *participatory*. Although staff clearly sought more active roles for learners in assessment, it was unclear during the first phase of the project when and how learners help to make that happen.

## Phases in the Development Process

In reflecting on the history of the project, we see our efforts to date as having proceeded through three phases that were not explicitly planned or anticipated and that were clearly not recognized as such while we were in the process. In describing these phases, we intend to provide a background for understanding the type of learner participation in assessment that evolved and some of its complexities and limitations.

*Sharing Knowledge and Constructing the Assessment Procedures.* Beginning with a simultaneous and mutual perception of need and interest, the Adult Literacy Evaluation Project (ALEP), as we call the collaboration between the Center for Literacy and the Literacy Research Center (LRC) at the University of Pennsylvania, set out to address a set of questions about the experiences of adults as learners and about assessment in adult literacy programs—who does it, for and with whom, with what methods, and for what outcomes or purposes. We met as a group in a seminar format—six staff members from CFL and six faculty and graduate students from LRC. Our goal was to design and use alternative procedures for assessment. At the time, we did not clarify the relationship between the procedures developed for the purposes of research and what CFL wanted for its day-to-day operations. We thought of ourselves as a practitioner or action research team with mutually agreed upon goals and a unique opportunity to learn and work together.

Reading and talking about experiences with adults, the group met weekly to recount the history of CFL assessment and to relate the concerns of staff about their current methods to new possibilities suggested by the literature. Adult learners were present only as silent partners whose needs and perspectives were represented for them by staff. Our efforts were directed toward creating a set of activities and relationships in which adults could be successful and demonstrate a range of abilities. This goal required procedures that were much more extensive and time-consuming than any used in the past and that stipulated new roles for staff coordinators. Following the traditions of interpretive or qualitative research, we tried to structure interviews to allow for improvisation so that the coordinator could follow the learner.

Over a period of five months, we constructed what we called the *initial planning conference* (IPC), an array of questions and activities designed to engage adults in self-exploration of their literacy practices and abilities. The IPC included opportunities to choose something of interest from among a collection of various types of reading material, to read selectively from photographs of signs in context, and to read and respond to narratives written by adults in the program that had been printed in a booklet for distribution at the initial interview. As part of the process of developing and revising these materials, we took a video-tape of a simulated IPC to a CFL student support group meeting in a neighborhood center and asked for their critique and response. The adults were vocal and articulate in their reactions—excited, for example, about the use of adult student–authored texts for reading material and impatient with what they regarded as some needlessly indirect questions and activities without clear purposes. Having incorporated their suggestions into yet another draft, several members of the CFL-LRC team piloted the procedures with adults who were asked not only to participate in the assessment procedures but to reflect on them as well. By documenting and discussing these experiences with adult learners, important changes were made in the assessment procedures.

The IPC and, six months later, the PC2 (Planning Conference Two) were participatory in several respects. Most important is the relationship between interviewer and adult. From the beginning, adults are intended not to be the objects of the assessment but rather the subjects or meaning makers in the process. Adults are assumed to be experts on their own knowledge and experience. Mistakes are viewed as partial successes (Lindfors, 1987), not as errors to be counted. Value is placed on the adults' perceptions of what makes reading and writing difficult and easy; the focus is on collaboration and coinvestigation. The initial interview is the first step in instruction, not a separate process of evaluation. Through discussion and reflection, adults come to understand their own capabilities, needs, and goals. While risk taking is encouraged, the adult learner makes the primary decisions about how much and what to do through choice of texts and tasks.

*Implementation and Critique.* At the end of the first phase of the project, the two coordinators who had taken part in designing the procedures made plans for using the assessment procedures with all incoming adults. Although implementation of the initial interview went smoothly, the introduction of the PC2 after six months coincided with the national literacy campaign and tremendous pressures on the agency to increase its services. Participants in the assessment project struggled with the need to meet with each adult still in the program for a second extended assessment interview while taking in many new students and matching them with appropriate tutors. Strains in the agency-university relationship began to surface as CFL attempted to cope with its day-to-day demands by shortening the assessment procedures and thus constraining the extent to which they could be learner-centered. CFL then decided to make the abbreviated IPC mandatory for coordinators across all areas of the city, including those who had not been involved in its construction. With increasing staff use of the IPC, it began to be apparent that conflicting ideologies within the agency made routine adoption of these assessment approaches problematic. Because of the complex nature of this kind of assessment and its underlying assumptions about literacy and learner centeredness, new staff needed much more than simply learning to administer these procedures if they were to use them. Even extensive discussion at the agency did not fully resolve important questions about the nature of reading and writing that are implicit in this approach to assessment and thus crucial to its success as an assessment tool. Resistance, retrenchment, and concerns about ownership began to emerge at CFL's staff meetings.

At the same time, project participants from the university began to focus on analyzing the data about adult learners that had been gathered from the original group in the study. In order to explore questions raised by this initial data, LRC decided with several active CFL students to conduct a series of ethnographic interviews focused on adults' perceptions of their own reading, writing, and learning. These interviews addressed what were felt to be important information gaps resulting from elliptical questions and the format of the shortened assessment procedures. While LRC moved to an interview style that was more participatory, CFL felt pressure to move in a somewhat different direction, driven by pragmatic needs related to service delivery.

Not only were LRC staff analyzing data without the expertise of CFL practitioners, but the assessment procedures designed collaboratively by the two groups began to be regarded by some at CFL as tools for research, not as procedures appropriate for day-to-day practice. Feeling overwhelmed by the sheer numbers of students and tutors, some of the staff at CFL began to see research as something that people at the university did and the original IPC as a research tool. Some began to make a distinction between their roles as practitioners and the roles of their LRC colleagues as researchers. Far from seeing the assessment procedure as a participatory process, some staff at CFL began to express concerns that the procedures were something "done to" learners in ways that were intrusive and that took advantage of them. To mandate that staff use a participatory process seems in retrospect contradictory, yet CFL by that time felt so strongly about opening up assessment procedures to increase learner involvement that a return to standardized forms of assessment was never considered.

As one might expect, the question of ownership of the assessment procedures began to emerge from these interactions. When conflict over the assessment occurred within CFL, the staff members who had been participants in the project from its inception began to feel strongly the need to explain and defend the participatory direction that the assessment had taken. CFL staff began to articulate even more clearly the rationale and theory behind it. These conversations eventually moved from assessment to a general unpacking of underlying assumptions about literacy and learning to the extent of learner participation in all aspects of the CFL program. CFL and LRC staff together began to talk about the possibility of increasingly collaborative forms of peer evaluation that could supplement the assessment interviews and about avenues for integrating assessment fully and meaningfully with teaching and learning. Concerns with the incongruence between alternative assessment on the one hand and traditional instruction and tutor training on the other also began to be discussed. It was becoming apparent that the movement toward participatory assessment processes had affected other parts of the agency's functioning. In the current phase, some of these issues have been further articulated, and new directions are beginning to emerge.

*Collaboration and Documentation for Outside Audiences.* CFL and LRC are now in the process of documenting the development of these assessment procedures so that they can be adapted for use by other literacy programs. The participating staff in the ALEP project, now doubled in size, has begun to articulate a clearer and more coherent philosophy for learner-centered assessment and its relationship to the rest of the program. Based in part what was learned from adults in the assessment process, plans are being made to revise tutor training and to gather systematic data about instruction in tutoring sessions and in classes. A joint CFL-LRC task force has been formed to reinvent tasks according to a newly revised conceptual framework, and current assessment procedures are being examined once again to see how adults can gain increasing control of the process. A small group of adult learners has come together to learn how to become tutors. These and other activities signal a period in the program's development in which new possibilities for learner participation are being initiated and explored. Although this phase has only just begun, it has made it possible for us to analyze what occurred and to draw from these experiences some observations and interpretations about learner involvement in assessment that we believe may be relevant to other settings.

## Issues and Directions in Learner-Centered Assessment

Through learners' participation in their own assessment, we see that standardized assessment fails to measure or even to recognize important strengths and knowledge brought to the learning situation that could play an integral role in instruction. Because the assessment procedure asks adult learners to discuss literacy practices and goals, reading and writing strategies, perceptions, and interests, these conversations often touch on intimate aspects of their lives. While some on the agency staff view these conversations as a means of helping adults become more active participants in their own learning, others view the interview as unnecessarily intrusive and a violation of personal privacy. This difference of opinion has highlighted several important issues. The first is that, more often than not in discussions about assessment procedures, staff speak in the name of learners. Although learners participate in their own assessment, they do not yet have a voice in critiquing and revising it. There is a growing concern with this situation as staff members talk more of the need for bringing students into various aspects of planning and program governance.

Among staff, there are a diverse set of beliefs about reading and writing, teaching and learning. Those who feel that the IPC is a successful means toward student-centered participatory learning are confident and comfortable with the idea that power can and should be shared in an educational setting, that teachers are not the experts and students the novices, and that inclusion in the learning process is not necessarily an intrusion. While those who are less comfortable with the IPC would not necessarily disagree with these principles, they argue that it does not (that it perhaps cannot) accomplish these goals. Moreover, they ask how these goals can be attained, arguing that differences of race, class, and culture often make it difficult for teachers and learners to act collaboratively. There are clear differences in beliefs about the practices of teaching and learning, and although we recognize the value of bringing such differences to light, it is not easy to resolve them. Some of what we have learned from the adults themselves has also been unsettling and goes unresolved. For example, when learners bring a view of literacy as a set of skills in decoding and spelling, our own biases and forms of assessment represent in some sense an imposition, however subtle, of another view— something that it is for us difficult to fully reconcile with the effort at learner centeredness.

Through the process of creating and recreating ways of assessing learning, of struggling to understand and compare perspectives on literacy and on teaching, this project has helped spread participatory learning throughout one literacy program. For some, the process has supported and extended their beliefs. For others, it has informed and educated. It has forced the whole agency to examine and compare its underlying assumptions and beliefs. By increasing the participation of adults in their own assessment, information has been gathered that supports a radical revision of tutor orientation and training and increased opportunity for adults both to tutor others and to structure their own learning.

Reflecting back on the project to envision its future directions, we wonder how adult learners can be more involved in program research and how adults can collaborate with each other to perform functions currently designated for the staff. We see the assessment process moving toward learner reading and writing portfolios that accumulate evidence of accomplishments and capabilities over time in all literacy-related life activities. These approaches to assessment seem more compatible with one-to-one tutoring when it is styled as collaborative learning and decision making and particularly with interdependent groups of adults organized to identify needed resources and plan the direction of their own instruction. Thus, participatory assessment becomes not just a way of measuring individual achievement but rather an opportunity to identify, with others, themes of importance in learners' lives and thus a catalyst to action that can alter the fundamental circumstances in which learners live.

## References

Eno, R. "Evaluation Evolution at the Center for Literacy." Unpublished manuscript, Center for Literacy, Philadelphia, 1985.

Fingeret, A. *Adult Literacy Education: Current and Future Directions.* Columbus, Ohio: ERIC Clearinghouse on Adult, Career, and Vocational Education, 1984.

Lindfors, J. *Children's Language and Learning.* (2nd ed.) Englewood Cliffs, N.J.: Prentice-Hall, 1987.

Lytle, S., and Schultz, K. "Assessing Literacy Learning with Adults: An Ideological Approach." In R. Beach and S. Hynds (eds.), *Becoming Readers and Writers During Adolescence and Adulthood.* Norwood, N.J.: Ablex, in press.

Reder, S. M. "Comparative Aspects of Functional Literacy Development: Three Ethnic Communities." In D. A. Wagner (ed.), *The Future of Literacy in a Changing World.* Oxford, England: Pergamon Press, 1987.

Scribner, S. "Introduction to Theoretical Perspectives on Comparative Literacy." In D. A. Wagner (ed.), *The Future of Literacy in a Changing World.* Oxford, England: Pergamon Press, 1987.

*Susan L. Lytle is director of the program in Reading/Writing/ Literacy at the Graduate School of Education, University of Pennsylvania, and associate director of the Literacy Research Center.*

*Alisa Belzer is a teacher and tutor trainer at the Center for Literacy in Philadelphia and a Master's candidate in Reading/ Writing/Literacy, University of Pennsylvania.*

*Katherine Schultz is a doctoral candidate in Reading/Writing/ Literacy, University of Pennsylvania.*

*Marie Vannozzi is lead coordinator at the Center for Literacy in Philadelphia and a Master's candidate in Reading/Writing/ Literacy, University of Pennsylvania.*

*The Academy, an alternative to traditional adult basic
education programs, is a learner-centered workplace literacy
program that engages adults in collaborative learning.*

# The Academy: A Learner-Centered Workplace Literacy Program

*Rena Soifer, Deborah L. Young,
Martha Irwin*

"All a man needed was a strong back and a coal shovel when I hired into the foundry thirty-seven years ago." Nate is talking about his early years as an autoworker. "No more though, no sir. Things has changed. Now I gotta be in some class all the time. All the time, just to keep up."

The offering of training and education to autoworkers is a recent trend. Until very recently, hourly work was structured so that line workers had little need to be skillful and thoughtful readers, writers, mathematicians, or computer users. Some workers, though schooled, had never really grasped the fundamentals of learning, some had left school at an early age to go to work, while others had forgotten the skills they once learned simply for lack of use. But the increasing use of electronic technology and the reorganization of work now require continuous education and retraining for Nate and many thousands of his fellow U.S. autoworkers. U.S. industry now faces the dilemma of having to retrain and reeducate a work force with diverse educational backgrounds.

A. Fingeret and P. Jurmo (eds.). *Participatory Literacy Education.*
New Directions for Continuing Education, no. 42. San Francisco: Jossey-Bass, Summer 1989.

**The Academy**

Eastern Michigan University (EMU) began the Academy in 1979 as an adult literacy project on the EMU campus funded by a federal Right-to-Read grant. The Academy developed a research-based, learner-centered approach aimed at upgrading the basic education of employed and unemployed adults within surrounding Washtenaw County.

In 1984, union and management at a nearby auto plant invited the Academy to set up a basic skills program for its hourly workers. Academy staff saw this as a new, challenging context in which to implement its learner-centered approach.

**Putting Philosophy into Practice**

The Academy's practices are based on knowledge about language, learning, thinking, teaching, and group dynamics culled from more than twenty-five years of research and theory in cognition, language, learning, psycholinguistics, and sociolinguistics. Three principles are basic to the Academy's approach: Learners' strengths are recognized and built on, teachers and learners collaborate as equal partners, and the environment has a significant impact on the quality of learning and teaching.

*Learners' Strengths.* One of the biggest challenges lies in guiding learners to be aware of the strengths that they have. Regardless of workers' earlier educational experiences, many have a poor self-concept. Years of working in a very directed, repetitive situation have only reinforced their low self-esteem and sense of powerlessness. Learners' low personal images have concealed their real abilities and learning capacities. Most undereducated adults have negative feelings about school learning and great uncertainty about their ability to learn "school things." In order for these people to move into the positive frame of mind necessary to become successful learners and improve their abilities to communicate and compute, they must confront and eliminate the feelings of inadequacy and failure.

We use the learners' language to initiate a process through which they begin to reconceptualize their views of themselves. Learners need to be reminded and reassured about their strengths—the things that they know and can do. They need to realize that they have accumulated skills, information, and experiences. They need to know that, in spite of their success or lack of success in past school learning, they are able to use the language that is necessary for personal relationships, work life, and community living.

*Collaboration.* Collaborative teaching and learning help to bring out learners' strengths. In order for collaboration to occur, learners meet in groups in which ideas can be shared and each group member, including the teacher, is a resource and support for every other person. The teaching must be both challenging and nonthreatening to stimulate interaction within the group and assist learners in overcoming self-doubts about their ability to learn. By participating in groups, learners receive reinforcement of what they know, and they come to see things from more than their own perspective. Learners also find out what they do not know and become receptive to new ideas.

In the group, learners discuss, read, and write about situations and provocative issues related to their personal and work lives. Staff select content materials to provoke powerful oral and written language from learners and, it is hoped, expand their knowledge of a particular topic. Some topics, such as work shift changes, are covered in a single session, while other topics are explored over several sessions. Health-related topics are discussed and written about during several sessions, which can include reading of materials on carpal tunnel syndrome, back problems, or other common worker ailments.

Open-ended questioning, justifying, clarifying, and examining issues from personal and collective perspectives engage learners in problem solving. Learners' views of themselves gradually but steadily improve as the teacher and other learners demonstrate genuine interest in their ideas through dialogue. They gain increased competence in their basic skills by putting their thoughts into words for a real audience. Then, putting their words onto paper and sharing the writings with the group arouse assertive and powerful language as they interact with one another. In this collaborative process, the teacher must act as a facilitator (Brookfield, 1986), not as an authority figure who knows and attempts to impart knowledge in the sequence and manner that he or she deems to be appropriate. An effective facilitator recognizes that "learning is a reciprocal process. As the teacher learns from the learners, so the learners learn from the teacher" (Hawkins, 1976, p. 9). Learners are encouraged to ask questions and agree or disagree with their peers and the facilitator. The teacher serves as a model, listening and accepting contributions from everyone. Learners realize that others are interested in their ideas and that it is safe to make mistakes.

*The Learning Environment.* The Academy teachers feel that the physical and psychological environment should convey a message of respect and offer a contrast to the noise and distractions of the workplace. Ideally, the learning center should be easily accessible to workers, and the classroom should be arranged so that groups of eight to ten adults can work comfortably together around a table. Essential teaching and learning materials, such as dictionaries, writing tablets, maps, and pencils are readily available and attractively arranged. The Academy also has its own library in the learning center, with additional shelves of books in cafeterias, break areas, and other worksite locations.

The instructional emphasis is on practicing "real" speaking, reading, and writing through doing rather than on learning about them. "One learns to read by reading and write by writing" (Smith, 1973, p. 195). The classroom environment creates a climate, and the teachers are the models. Everyone—teachers and students—reads and writes.

The psychological climate is especially crucial since there is personal risk when adults return to the classroom. We have found that small-group settings are ideal for helping learners to build peer support and increase their self-esteem by allowing them to take advantage of the knowledge of each group member. Not only does the group setting provide language practice, but it simulates the settings—quality circles, self-directed work groups, collaborative work teams—that are becoming standard procedure in many workplaces today. The learner gradually begins to transfer some of the group processes learned in the classroom to work groups and family relationships. As the learners begin to walk taller, hold their heads higher, and speak more succinctly, they are encouraged to take part in additional activities in the Academy program: Individuals serve as hosts and speakers at large biannual awards ceremonies, they volunteer to be interviewed by reporters, and they contribute articles to various publications. Besides letters to the editors of local newspapers and to government representatives, workers write for the union's *Local 849 News*, management's *Factory Street Journal*, the Poet's Corner in the *Ypsilanti Press*, and the *Mountain Laurel*—a monthly journal about mountain life published in Virginia.

### Instruction

Our learners' needs determine the ways in which we schedule classes, choose materials, deliver instruction, and integrate technology.

*Scheduling.* Classes are scheduled before and after work shifts. The classes meet for one-and-a-half hours twice a week. All classes are scheduled for eight-week periods—a sharp contrast to the drop-in arrangements common at industrial learning centers. Regular and continuous instruction and practice are important for any learning, whether it involves skiing or keyboarding. We have found that scheduled sessions allow learners to commit themselves for a predetermined time period. Teacher and learners confer to review learners' work at the end of each eight-week session, and the learner then decides whether to continue, move on to another class, or not return.

*Materials.* Because the learners' ideas and experiences form the basis for the instructional program, authentic materials must be used. By *authentic materials* we mean newspaper articles, magazines, and visuals (pictures, films, cartoons, and the like) that build on prior knowledge and relate to the learners' personal and work lives. Materials on provocative topics are deliberately chosen for their connections with important work, social, and political issues. Staff keep themselves informed of current workplace issues through shop talk with workers and by reading newsletters and other materials dealing with industry concerns. From discussion of these high-interest topics, learners generate writings that are then used for further instruction. The teacher uses these materials to create real-life language learning situations in which reading and writing activities have specific purposes. Searching manuals for information about equipment or writing letters to companies that supply the plant are just two examples of the work-related reading and writing that takes place in Academy classrooms.

*Learning Strategies.* For the Academy, the purpose of instruction is to help learners develop their own learning strategies. Useful strategies include predicting, previewing, connecting ideas with previous experiences, questioning, and summarizing. The teacher teaches specific strategies, models them, and provides opportunities for guided practice. When introducing a strategy, the teacher explains what it is, how it is done, and when it is best used. The teacher models the strategy in all instruction so that learners see it used consistently. Learners practice it with different materials until it becomes their own.

*Technology.* "A work force that has learned how to learn is one of the most important competitive levers an organization can have in an environment of ongoing technological change" (Schuck, 1985, p. 139). It would be unrealistic and unfair to teach basic skills to industrial workers and exclude the use of technology. However, it is important to make sure both that the way in which computers are used and that what is taught about computers are relevant to the learner and consistent with sound principles of instruction.

The Academy does not use computers for independent drill and practice on discrete skills or to manage instruction through computerized testing. We use software that is congruent with a learner-centered program: word processors, data bases, spreadsheets, and graphics. The word processors and data bases are the most versatile. With word processors, learners can enter and edit their own texts, and the teacher can create personalized activities, such as open-ended sentences and guided writing. Data bases provide opportunities for creating and accessing collections of data about any topic of interest to the learner. Most often their selection is about a personal or work experience that has a connection with technology. Learners have also created data bases about the parts used in their work, their coworkers' car preferences, or their favorite foods or restaurants. Learners use these data to draw conclusions and make generalizations. In other words, the computer is simply another tool in class that can augment learners' listening, speaking, reading, and writing activities. We are not teaching about computers. We are helping learners to become comfortable with using computers to perform meaningful tasks.

## Evaluation

Evaluation is the most troubling and persistent problem that the Academy has faced. One of the main reasons is that adult basic education programs have traditionally been measured by numerical scores on standardized tests. Funders of workplace literacy programs often demand numerical data as a measure of a program's success. However, standardized tests cannot satisfactorily assess the affective and cognitive results from the Academy's instructional approach. Such measures are inappropriate for adults in that they do not account for the effects of adult life and work experiences. Although the tasks measured by these tests have been standardized on adult populations, they do not reflect the tasks performed in real life. Since they are inappropriate for adults, it is important to have other means of assessing learner progress.

Evaluation is much broader than testing. Evaluation is an ongoing process that uses a number of indicators and involves both teachers and learners. A portfolio of measurements is a much more comprehensive way of assessing learning than a test score. The primary purpose of evaluation—to enable learners and teachers to be aware of progress—must be constantly kept in mind. In the Academy, we evaluate as a means of celebrating learners' successes.

In a learner-centered program, learners monitor their own progress. The Academy learners do this in a number of ways: They graph their spelling successes, list the books they have read, record and date their writings, and track their attendance. Learners regularly write anecdotal records of incidents that are related to the Academy classes.

In addition, learners complete pre and post reading-behavior questionnaires that assess the reading strategies they use. Pre and post writing assessments consist of actual writings that are evaluated for authenticity, organization, and mechanics. These somewhat more formal measures are reviewed together by learner and teacher.

Affective factors are extremely important, but they can only be assessed informally. Self-concept has a powerful influence on how successful learners are. However, it cannot be measured or quantified. The best way of assessing significant affective changes is through observations by the teacher and, more important, through learners' growing feelings of confidence and power.

## Recommendations

For a learner-centered approach to work in an industrial setting, communication, preparation, and commitment are necessary. This section discusses some of the associated concerns.

Misunderstanding between the educational provider and the funder can cause delays and block a program's success. In a workplace program, labor, management, and teachers should plan together. Such collaboration builds on the resources of everyone and sends a loud, clear message to workers and management that education plays a significant part in the manufacturing of quality products. When everyone has contributed resources, whether they be ideas or space, he or she feels a sense of ownership and responsibility for success. People understand that it is a team effort.

One example of collaboration between labor, management, and teachers occurred in the beginning weeks of the Academy's first industrial program. For recruitment purposes, the staff recognized the need to meet and talk with workers, explain the program, and answer questions. Within three weeks a plan was developed whereby all workers were scheduled to meet as groups with teachers to talk about the program. This would not have been possible without joint discussions and planning.

Another way of increasing the effectiveness of the teaching-learning process is to have the teachers learn about labor history, the plant culture, and the work that is being done in the plant where they will be teaching. Teachers will feel more comfortable and more knowledgeable about the worksite if labor and management personnel give them some orientation to these topics before classes begin. Once teachers have started teaching, they need to go routinely out on the shop floor to increase their understanding of how instruction can be related to the work situation.

Introduction to the worksite is only one part of teacher preparation for workplace literacy. Teachers must be carefully selected for their understanding of adult learning; for their understanding of the connections between listening, speaking, reading, and writing; and for their preparation in specific content areas. There should be continuous in-service training and available supervision, particularly in learning to facilitate small groups in a learner-centered classroom.

Perhaps one of the biggest challenges for educational providers is to hold on to what they believe and act on those beliefs. Good teaching and learning are hard work, and adult educators face many issues and problems, not the least of which are people who misunderstand or ignore the implications of learner centeredness. Everyone who is concerned with workplace literacy—management, unions, teachers, and learners—must get used to the idea of workers who can think, make decisions, and contribute.

To keep us on track, we need to keep an eye on our learners. Their success will provide the inspiration and guidance that we need to continue our important work.

72

## References

Brookfield, S. D. *Understanding and Facilitating Adult Learning: A Comprehensive Analysis of Principles and Effective Practices.* San Francisco: Jossey-Bass, 1986.

Hawkins, T. *Group Inquiry Techniques for Teaching Adults.* Urbana, Ill.: National Council of Teachers of English, 1976.

Schuck, G. "Intelligent Technology, Intelligent Workers: A New Pedagogy for the High-Tech Workplace." *Organizational Dynamics,* 1985, *14*, 128–140.

Smith, F. *Psycholinguistics and Reading.* New York: Holt, Rinehart & Winston, 1973.

*Rena Soifer is the specialist for workplace education with the Corporate Services Center of Eastern Michigan University in Ypsilanti, Michigan.*

*Deborah L. Young is a technology specialist at Eastern Michigan University Academy in Ypsilanti, Michigan.*

*Martha Irwin is a professor of teacher education at Eastern Michigan University in Ypsilanti, Michigan.*

*A small number of innovative, community-based organizations
and volunteer literacy groups have taken the lead in developing
participatory literacy education practices in the United States.*

# History in the Making:
# Key Players in the Creation
# of Participatory Alternatives

*Paul Jurmo*

The participatory thinking and practice described in Chapters One
through Seven are at this point generally not widely used in the literacy
field. However, interest in the participatory approach seems to be growing among literacy providers and support institutions. This chapter,
which is based on Chapter Three of Jurmo (1987), surveys key players in
the creation of participatory alternatives.

## The Literacy Providers

The segments of the literacy field that have shown the most interest
in the participatory approach to date are the community-based organizations and the volunteer literacy field. A few promising signs of interest
are also evident within the workplace literacy field. Little evidence of

For their help in providing additional, updated information for this chapter,
the author wishes to thank Al Bennett, Marty Finsterbusch, Gregg Jackson, Virginia Lawson, Jonathan McKallip, Phil Rose, and Peter Waite. This chapter is
based on Jurmo, 1987, Chapter Three.

A. Fingeret and P. Jurmo (eds.). *Participatory Literacy Education.*
New Directions for Continuing Education, no. 42. San Francisco: Jossey-Bass, Summer 1989.

support for a participatory approach could be found in Adult Basic Education, correctional education, or other segments of the field.

*Community-Based Programs.* The Association for Community Based Education (ACBE) defines *community-based organizations* (CBOs) as "groups set up to serve a given geographical area and constituency—usually urban or rural poverty communities and the educationally, economically, and socially disadvantaged. They are formed by their constituencies—including . . . ethnic, racial and cultural minorities—to meet specific needs that exist within the community. Their goals inevitably go beyond the mere provision of educational services to missions of individual and community empowerment. They often link education to community development activities. Their methodological approaches are nontraditional, to meet the needs of those whom traditional education has failed, and learner-centered, focused on helping people meet objectives they themselves set in response to their own needs" (Association for Community Based Education, n.d., pp. 2–3).

Under this definition, CBOs inherently involve learners in defining their own needs and use learner-centered means to respond to those needs. They do so both to enhance the personal development of learners and to change the communities within which the learners live in positive ways.

In fact, these kinds of CBOs have led in the use of participatory literacy education from the earliest days of literacy work in the United States. During the civil rights movement, community organizers ran literacy classes in the South to enable black residents to pass the literacy test that was required in order to become a registered voter. Classes used the voter registration test materials as a key instructional text and involved learners in discussions of human rights and other community issues. For many learners, the final exam was a trip to the voting registration office where they would attempt to pass the literacy test that prevented them from exercising the fundamental right of voting (Adams and Horton, 1975; Morris, n.d.).

By the 1980s, similar social-change-oriented CBOs were cited in several national reports for their particular effectiveness in serving hard-to-reach communities (Harman and Hunter, 1985; "CBOs: Reaching the Hardest to Reach," 1986). But little research has been done on CBOs, in large part because these overburdened groups have had little time to devote to the documentation of their experience for others. For these and other reasons, there is limited systematic information on the number of CBOs or on what makes them effective.

To a limited degree, the Washington, D.C.–based ACBE serves as a link among these groups. The association provides modest funding in the form of minigrants, and it developed an evaluation system for CBOs. It hosts an annual conference, lobbies for CBOs on Capitol Hill, publishes a directory and newsletters, and conducts community-level training workshops for literacy organizations that are interested in developing a participatory approach. The ACBE literacy effort received a substantial boost from the MacArthur Foundation in 1987 in the form of a grant for $750,000. In 1986, MacArthur funded Push Literacy Action Now, a Washington, D.C., CBO, to produce a position paper on the need for a national learner-centered effort. These grants have made MacArthur the largest single source of funding for participatory efforts to date.

*Volunteer Programs.* During the period between 1984 and 1989, both Laubach Literacy Action (LLA) and Literacy Volunteers of America (LVA) began to look more closely at the kinds of participatory practice described in Chapters Three through Seven. In part this interest emerged from the positive leadership provided by local volunteer programs, which on their own had gotten learners involved in conferences, support groups, and other activities. At the same time, volunteer groups were under considerable pressure from advocates of the participatory approach who criticized volunteer program instructional and management approaches as ineffective and patronizing.

*Laubach Literacy Action.* The years 1983 and 1984 marked the beginning of LLA's interest in the issue of student involvement. Students were talking to the media and making their presence felt at LLA national headquarters. At the same time, some LLA personnel were considering how social-change literacy efforts in the Third World might be adapted to U.S. programs.

In 1984, an event occurred that served as a catalyst for much of LLA's subsequent student involvement efforts. Lutheran Church Women covered the costs of sending fifty students from local LLA programs to Laubach's 1984 biennial conference. This experience was deemed successful in laying the groundwork for further peer support among learners, which was seen by some as an extension of LLA's "Each One Teach One" philosophy. Building on this experience, LLA arranged to have about sixty students attend its 1986 biennial conference, this time with no travel subsidies provided. Learners ran workshops and recommended the formation of a national LLA student network linked by a student newsletter and state representatives.

In response, LLA created a national student newsletter and assembled a four-member team of student leaders. This team urged LLA to foster local student support groups, expand learners' roles beyond their traditional roles in tutoring relationships, see empowerment as a goal for learners, and protect learners who "go public" from embarrassment.

This same student advisory group then helped put together a national student congress that was held in Philadelphia in September 1987 for fifty students from Laubach affiliates nationwide. The congress produced statements on the issues identified by the student advisory committee. These statements were widely circulated among LLA affiliates and inspired a growth during 1988 in student involvement in support groups and public awareness activities. LLA students were particularly visible in the Learner of the Month public-service messages aired that year on ABC. These same learners appeared on stage with Barbara Bush during a National Literacy Honors extravaganza at the Washington Hilton.

By 1989, the national student advisory committee was being more formally established as an official New Readers Committee comprised of five learners deemed by LLA to be outstanding local leaders. This committee was to represent student concerns before the national LLA steering committee, one of whose elected members was, for the first time, a former LLA student. And a second national congress was planned for September 1989, this time to include learners from Literacy Volunteers of America programs as well.

By early 1989, LLA hoped to conduct a national survey to document how many of its local programs were involving learners in these ways. It also planned to put together a series of resource materials for those wishing to implement various student activities.

Nevertheless, for LLA, student involvement was almost exclusively on the management side of the program. In the area of instruction, LLA was telling local affiliates to feel free to adapt non-LLA instructional approaches to their curricula. But apart from a guidebook or two on topics like language experience (Kennedy and Roeder, 1975), LLA was not making significant efforts to provide affiliates with the kinds of participatory instructional tools described in Chapters Three through Seven. LLA thus exposed itself to the criticism that, although its learner support activities had perhaps been successful in providing a comfortable "home" for learners, it was not developing the more effective instructional tools represented in whole-language and other learner-centered approaches. A number of Laubach affiliates began communicating with participatory programs to discuss how they might replace their traditional Laubach methodology with a more learner-centered approach.

*Literacy Volunteers of America.* LVA traces its interest in creating new roles for learners to the late 1970s when a Connecticut affiliate arranged to have a student coach counsel fellow students and act as a go-between between students and staff. This nontraditional student role was subsequently disseminated as a model that other LVA affiliates were invited to try. By the early 1980s, the issue of student involvement was being discussed at LVA national conferences, and reports began reaching LVA headquarters of learner participation in tutor training, intake procedures, dropout prevention efforts, and advisory groups.

LVA's Field Services Committee published *Student Involvement Guidelines* (Literacy Volunteers of America, 1984), which documented this growing interest and recommended that programs consider involving learners in most of the management activities described in Chapters Three through Seven. LVA's emerging interest in student involvement was pushed forward by a special grant. In 1986, author Sidney Sheldon gave $10,000 to LVA to be used for special student-related activities.

Half of the grant money was set aside to cover travel costs for students set to attend LVA's national conferences in 1986 and 1987. At these conferences, learners for the first time went beyond the mere giving of testimonials. They put together special presentations for the general conference audience, organized workshops for themselves, and prepared recommendations for consideration by LVA headquarters.

At the 1986 national conference, the LVA national office awarded the remaining $5,000 of the Sidney Sheldon grant, augmented by $2,000 from Lutheran Church Women, to thirteen affiliates for special student projects. Small grants supported local student councils, student newsletters, a student telephone committee, book clubs, student coaches, and a parent-child reading circle. LVA subsequently continued this series of grants, receiving twenty-five proposals in 1987 and fifty applications in 1988. In its most recent grants, LVA emphasized that projects not be merely for students but be managed by students.

A revision of *Student Involvement Guidelines* based on responses from 100 local affiliates to a questionnaire was issued in 1989. The responses showed that interest in the notion of student involvement had grown among affiliates: In the 1984 survey, 67 percent of the responding affiliates said that learners should be more widely involved; in 1988, 85 percent responded in this way.

By early 1989, LVA headquarters felt that many new affiliates were building the notion of student involvement into their programs right from the start. This change in mindset at the local level—seeing learners as fully participating members of the organization—was seen as vital to LVA's effort to shift to the learner-centered approach. A similar shift in thinking was also evident at the national level, where board members had learned from the students who had taken part in the national conferences and were paying increasingly active attention to learners' concerns.

Again at the national level, LVA by 1989 was consciously incorporating whole-language principles into its curriculum development work. In 1988 and 1989, it developed a manual on small-group instruction that encouraged affiliates to take advantage of the peer support that such groups can afford. Affiliates that had been reluctant to try small groups were reported to have become enthusiastic when they saw the format demonstrated in workshops. The fact that LVA founder Ruth Colvin adopted the format in her parent-literacy project has further legitimized the idea for affiliates attached to the traditional one-to-one format.

In its tutor-training activities, by 1989 LVA was trying to present small groups, the language experience approach, and its other methods as only tools to be used in a larger process. That process, LVA increasingly emphasized, was to begin with the students. Instruction should focus on identifying learner goals and motivations and on selecting the techniques that respond to them. These ideas met with acceptance from many of the retired schoolteachers who volunteer as LVA tutors. Traditionally, many of these schoolteachers were wedded to the old ways, in which the teacher feeds information to students. Now it seemed that increasing numbers of teachers had received training in the whole-language philosophy and they had thus been prepared to listen to LVA's ideas for a more learner-centered curriculum. LVA feels that such shifts are in keeping with LVA's founding principles of providing tutors with the best tools possible. In this case, learner-centered instructional methodologies have been officially recognized as effective tools.

*Other Literacy Providers.* There is little evidence that participatory learning has caught on in any significant way in other segments of the literacy field. However, workplace literacy efforts have at once shown real promise and presented significant obstacles for advocates of a participatory approach.

As workplace literacy became a focus of attention during the late 1980s, claims were made that employers wanted workers who could apply basic reading, writing, and math skills to real-life problems; think critically and take initiative to solve problems; and work in teams—all key elements of the kinds of participatory thinking cited in Chapter Two of this volume. Widely circulated manuals (Business Council for Effective Literacy, 1987; U.S. Department of Education, 1988; Sticht, 1987) and reports (*A Job to Be Done,* 1987; Carnevale, Gainer, and Meltzer, 1988; Petrini, 1989) on workplace literacy proposed the contextualized learning approach as a solution to these workplace needs. A minority of workplace programs—including the programs described in Chapters Four and Seven—took these principles to heart and involved learners in developing worker-centered curricula based on interests taken from their workplaces and lives.

However, at the field level most workplace literacy programs appeared to consist of traditional basic skills programs applied in a workplace setting. The fact that a contextualized approach was not being used was often due to a lack of professional and other resources required to tailor a program to the situation of particular workers. However, in some cases, textbook, software, and video manufacturers used their marketing clout to promote their own decontextualized approaches to employers looking for a quick solution for their employees' basic skills problems.

Thus, while the interest in workplace literacy provided an opportunity to investigate at least some principles of the participatory approach, the resources needed to translate the discussions into creation of participatory practice were often lacking.

**Support Institutions**

Support institutions are organizations in the literacy field that supply literacy providers with various kinds of resources. These organizations provide the field with planning and coordination, funding and in-kind assistance, research and evaluation, public awareness, and training and instructional materials. Except for the support from the MacArthur Foundation, Lutheran Church Women, Sidney Sheldon, and workplace literacy research cited earlier, there is limited evidence that support institutions have a significant, ongoing interest in developing the participatory approach.

For example, a few national, state, and local coalitions have learners on their boards, or put the topic of student involvement on their list of issues to be discussed, or hosted student-recognition events. Similarly, some public awareness campaigns have had students provide personal testimonials. A few national, state, and local coalitions have allowed learners to discuss student issues and make recommendations to literacy policy makers.

Funding sources likewise provided limited support for student newsletters and anthologies, support groups, and student conferences. The U.S. Department of Education's National Diffusion Network funded Bronx Educational Services to disseminate its community-based model nationwide. Federal VISTA funds enabled outstanding literacy students to stay on in their programs as paraprofessional staff. The research community has developed some learner-centered assessment tools like the University of Pennsylvania's ALEP project (see Chapter Six) and the California State Library's CALPEP project. A few university-based adult education programs have established courses for practitioners interested in developing their participatory thinking and practice. Within the publishing world, a few companies have published the kinds of theoretical works cited in Chapter Two, but the use of these works tends to be confined to university-level education courses. With its *ESL for Action* (Auerbach and Wallerstein, 1987), Addison-Wesley was one of the few commercial publishers providing literacy practitioners with learner-centered instructional tools. World Education, with its *Focus on Basics Newsletter* (World Education, 1987-89), and an underground of participatory-minded programs occasionally produced learner-centered teachers' guides and learner-written reading materials, but these texts had limited circulation within the literacy field.

**Conclusion**

At the close of the 1980s, supporters of the participatory approach can point to growth in learner-centered activity not only among social-change-oriented CBOs but among some mainstream programs and support institutions as well. In fact, a few mainstream groups have jettisoned traditional approaches entirely and taken on new identities as participatory programs. But these positive examples of programs in transition are exceptions in the literacy field.

More commonly, attention and resources continued to be devoted to traditional thinking and practice, whether packaged as workbooks or in high-tech formats. Participatory educators thus have reason to be both encouraged and discouraged as they look ahead to the new decade.

## References

Adams, F., with Horton, M. *Unearthing Seeds of Fire: The Idea of Highlander.* Winston-Salem, N.C.: John F. Blair, 1975.

Association for Community-Based Education. "A Project to Strengthen Community Based Adult Literacy Programs." Washington, D.C.: Association for Community Based Education. Funding proposal, n.d.

Auerbach, E., and Wallerstein, N. *ESL for Action: Problem Posing at Work.* Reading, Mass: Addison-Wesley, 1987.

Business Council for Effective Literacy. *Job-Related Basic Skills: A Guide for Planners of Employee Programs.* New York: Business Council for Effective Literacy, 1987.

Carnevale, A. P., Gainer, L. J., and Meltzer, A. S. *Workplace Basics: The Skills Employers Want.* Alexandria, Va.: American Society for Training and Development, 1988.

"CBOs: Reaching the Hardest to Reach." *BCEL [Business Council for Effective Literacy] Newsletter,* April 1986, p. 1.

Harman, D., and Hunter, C.S.J. *Adult Illiteracy in the United States.* (2nd ed.) New York: McGraw-Hill, 1985.

*A Job to Be Done.* Pittsburgh, Penn.: WQED-Pittsburgh. (PBS documentary aired October 1987.)

Jurmo, P. J. "Learner Participation Practices in Adult Literacy Efforts in the United States." Unpublished Ed.D. dissertation, University of Massachusetts, Amherst, 1987.

Kennedy, K., and Roeder, S. *Using Language Experience with Adults: A Guide for Teachers.* Syracuse, N.Y.: New Readers Press, 1975.

Literacy Volunteers of America. *Student Involvement Guidelines.* Syracuse, N.Y.: Literacy Volunteers of America, 1984.

Literacy Volunteers of America. *Student Involvement Guidelines.* Syracuse, N.Y.: Literacy Volunteers of America, 1989.

Morris, A. D. *The Origins of the Civil Rights Movement: Black Communities Organizing for Change.* New York: Free Press, 1984.

Petrini, C. (ed.). "Four by Four: How Can Businesses Fight Workplace Illiteracy?" *Training and Development Journal,* January 1989, pp. 18–24.

Sticht, T. G. *Functional Context Education Workshop Resource Notebook.* San Diego, Calif.: Applied Behavioral and Cognitive Sciences, 1987.

U.S. Department of Education. *The Bottom Line: Basic Skills in the Workplace.* Washington, D.C.: U.S. Department of Education and U.S. Department of Labor, 1988.

World Education. *Focus on Basics Newsletter.* Boston: World Education, 1987–1989.

*Paul Jurmo is senior program associate at the Business Council for Effective Literacy in New York City.*

*A national literacy effort built on participatory principles will require study of existing learner-centered theory and practice, resource development, research and development, training and networking, and careful planning.*

# What Needs to Be Done to Build Participatory Alternatives

*Paul Jurmo*

Those who are interested in building a participatory approach to literacy education in the United States have solid foundation stones with which to work. These building blocks consist of the considerable theoretical and practical work that thoughtful and committed researchers, practitioners, and learners have already carried out.

But these building blocks have not yet been joined together to form a solid foundation for an effective national movement. Participatory theory and practice remain scattered and isolated across the literacy field.

And to further complicate matters, the literacy field is itself not very solid. With its limited vision and resources, it is an unstable environment

This chapter updates Chapters Five and Six of Jurmo (1987). For their special help, the author's gratitude and admiration go to Al Bennett, Beverly Campbell, Jacqueline Cook, Jon Deveaux, Art Ellison, Marty Finsterbusch, Mike Fox, Karen Griswold, George Hagenauer, Greg Hart, Paul Ilsley, Michael James, Marti Lane, Jane McGovern, Jonathan McKallip, Bo Montgomery, Guitele Nicoleau, Nancy Oakley, Maria Quiroga, Phil Rose, Kathy Reilly, Klaudia Rivera, Pancho Rivera, Ira Shor, Rena Soifer, Ellen Steiner, Gabriele Strohschen, Carole Talan, Peter Waite, and Nina Wallerstein.

A. Fingeret and P. Jurmo (eds.). *Participatory Literacy Education.*
New Directions for Continuing Education, no. 42. San Francisco: Jossey-Bass, Summer 1989.

in which to work. This instability discourages anyone attempting to develop a sustained, unified effort within the field.

So, for those with a participatory perspective, a key question remains: What needs to be done to build participatory education as a real force in the adult literacy field? More than fifty supporters of the approach were presented with that question. The recommendations that follow are built on their responses and on the evidence cited in the previous chapters.

### Recommendation 1: Form Study Teams

Practitioners, learners, and others who are interested in building a participatory alternative in the literacy field should develop study teams of like-minded people from their own programs and perhaps from other programs. Team members can pool their resources to carry out the thinking and action that will be needed. The teams can also build the morale and group identity needed to sustain the effort through the long and complex process ahead.

### Recommendation 2: Build Bridges to Develop a
### Deeper Understanding of Participatory Literacy Education

Without an understanding of what is meant by participatory literacy education, it is unlikely that practice will be strengthened or that the participatory approach will be a significant force in the literacy field. Those interested in developing such an understanding need to find the time to examine their own thinking vis-à-vis participatory education as well as the thinking of others. For example, the research described in earlier chapters should be widely discussed and analyzed. The levels of learner participation should be understood, and the arguments that support active learner involvement should be studied carefully.

For example, the efficiency argument generally comes from whole-language work done at the school level and from contextualized work done in the workplace segment of the adult literacy field. As such, the valuable theory and practice developed in these areas have generally been isolated from most adult literacy practitioners and policy makers. To allow this valuable research to be disseminated in the adult literacy field as a whole, new training opportunities must be created. But at the same time efficiency advocates should recognize that personal and social issues also have an impact on student learning.

Humanistic education has developed methods for group learning and brainstorming and other means of enhancing learners' self-confidence, social skills, and problem solving. These methods could be of great use to those looking for practical techniques for getting students involved in the learning process.

At the same time, personal development advocates should consider the social-change argument that collective action is necessary to change the conditions shaping the learner's life. Personal development supporters—especially those whose background in reading and writing instruction is limited—might also expand their literacy instruction abilities through study of work done by whole-language supporters.

Although social-change supporters are vocal in their calls for support for the participatory approach, they often remain aloof from the rest of the literacy field. The cause of this aloofness varies from individual to individual. But it is likely to be due to some combination of burnout, despair, cynicism, elitism, and lack of time or to the rational conclusion that outreach to other groups drains resources away from more immediate needs. Whatever the cause, this aloofness prevents social-change advocates from learning from the thinking and practice of others. It also prevents social-change supporters from winning converts to the social-change position and thereby continues to limit social-change efforts to a few widely cited but isolated programs and writers.

To remedy this situation, social-change advocates need to broaden the range of theoretical work that they study. And they need to make concerted efforts to reach out to others who do not fully understand or support the social-change position but who might nonetheless be sympathetic to the basic notion of active roles for learners.

No single, unified theory will emerge from this process of communication among proponents of the various perspectives on active learner participation. What should instead be the goal is for all interested parties to develop their own understanding of the purposes that a participatory approach can serve. By so doing, they might discover new allies and new tools.

### Recommendation 3: Beware of Contextual Constraints

Participatory efforts operate in larger contexts that are not generally supportive of the idea that illiterate adults are capable of exercising power. Advocates of a participatory approach must be prepared to deal constructively with political constraints, demands for accountability, and economic constraints.

*Political Constraints.* Advocates of participatory literacy must understand how power is distributed in society at large and within and among literacy programs themselves and be prepared to deal with resistance to the notion of creating roles with power for low-level readers. For example, low-level readers may themselves be reluctant to take on new roles because the very notion of shaping an educational institution is foreign to them. They have grown up in a society that, notwithstanding its founding principles of democracy, does not give most people much opportunity to participate in decision making in the schools, workplaces, social services, and other major institutions that adults encounter regularly. Many learners have also had experiences in adult education programs structured in traditional ways that do not encourage participatory roles for learners. They are likely to feel bewildered—and perhaps threatened—by participatory efforts asking them to take on new responsibilities.

Even when learners are willing to take on new, more participatory roles, they may encounter resistance from fellow students or from family members, friends, or employers. These others may not be willing to accept the newly empowered learners' new identity, because it challenges familiar power relationships.

In addition, when staff open the decision-making process up to students, there might be confusion about how to manage all the suggestions and demands that begin to flood in. And the high-level decision makers who control adult education and other institutions may view a shift in control as a threat to the vested interests and the current power structure. High-level officials may move to limit the resources available to participatory programs.

Participatory programs may themselves encounter resentment and outright hostility from segments of the literacy field that see them as competitors for the scarce resources available.

To deal constructively with these political complexities, advocates of participatory literacy need to take a carrot and stick approach. The carrot can take the form of reasoned explanations of the benefits that participatory approach can produce for learners, the literacy field, communities, the economy, and the democratic process. Funders should be shown that support for effective learner-centered programs is a sound way of using their funds and that it will ultimately reflect on them in positive ways.

Participatory advocates should also pull together all their allies—learners, practitioners, community members, and others—to create a power bloc—a critical mass—of learner-centered activists. To accomplish this, advocates will have to be willing to compromise, communicate, find areas of agreement, and sometimes agree to disagree with others who nonetheless have shown an interest in learner-centered education. The resulting solidarity can, if necessary, serve as a stick that advocates of participatory approaches can use to convince unsupportive institutions of the power that these approaches represent.

*Demands for Accountability.* Accountability is a two-edged sword. Unreceptive funders can use it to push participatory programs toward inappropriate standards. But it can also be a tool that funders, practitioners, and learners can use to improve participatory practice.

To date, participatory programs have generally had to deal with the negative side of the accountability issue, which occurs when funders require them to use standardized reading tests, enrollment figures, and other traditional means to measure program success. Participatory programs do not consider these assessment tools to be an appropriate means of measuring what learner-centered efforts try to accomplish. So they tend to feel that being forced to use these measures is at the least an imposition and at the worst an attempt to push them into adopting traditional literacy practices.

In some cases, learner-centered programs go along with these demands and submit their staffs and learners to standardized tests and other required reporting procedures. However, some of these programs keep records of their own based on assessments that they consider to be more useful. These measures can include informal feedback from learners, periodic review of learning contracts, observation of student involvement levels in various activities, student learning logs, and other methods developed by whole-language researchers and ethnographers.

If funders are truly interested in determining how successful literacy programs are, they need to take time to reassess what they should be funding and to work with effective programs to develop appropriate measures of program achievement. Participatory programs need to take the time to explain their instructional and assessment methods to funders as a way of helping to shape the field.

Learner-centered practitioners must also be prepared to argue their case before another group: the learners themselves. Learners invest a lot of themselves in their programs, and quite legitimately they want to be sure that their investment is well spent. Learners who have become accustomed to measuring programs by performance on standardized tests will have to be involved in discussions about the instructional and assessment methods used by participatory programs.

*Economic Constraints.* Both learners and practitioners who support the idea of learner participation are faced by difficult economic choices. Learners frequently need to drop out of literacy programs for financial reasons, and practitioners are faced with similar decisions. Unfortunately, few adult literacy instructors in the United States are presently paid a salary that is adequate to support a family. Literacy programs themselves generally continue to operate on shoestring budgets that barely cover their short-term basic operating expenses, let along staff training and other long-term development needs.

A major effort must be made to develop financial and other resources. Learner-centered advocates must first identify the goals that they hope to accomplish in the future and then the resources that they will need in order to achieve those goals. Basic operating costs—including equitable wages and benefits for professional staff and for learners working on staff—must be covered. Funds will also have to be available for new expenses incurred as a result of increased learner participation and for support services like daycare, transportation, and counseling. Programs must decide how many of these activities they want to take on and prepare a budget.

Learner-centered programs must then identify potential sources of funding. Information on funders actively or potentially open to learner-centered programs can be developed from formal sources like nonprofit funding directories and from informal information networks of nonprofit agencies.

Activists must then develop short- and long-term strategies for enlisting resources from these funders. In the short term, they must submit funding proposals that have the dual aims of raising funds for effective projects and of informing funding sources about the potential in learner-centered practice. In the long run, activists must become advocates, arguing the case for a participatory approach before funders and legitimizing it as an effective alternative that deserves support. As noted in earlier chapters, learners themselves are some of the best advocates for participatory education.

Resource development goes beyond the securing of additional funds. Activists can work with community colleges, teacher training institutions, and universities, which can provide valuable research, training, and networking services. The media can provide coverage for effective participatory efforts. Publishers can prepare and disseminate theoretical and practically oriented texts for learners and practitioners. And the American public as a whole—particularly the young educated class—can provide volunteers, funding, and other forms of support. It is up to learner-centered activists to figure out ways of tapping these resources.

**Recommendation 4: Institute a Research and Development System**

Participatory educators need a systematic and sustained research and development system. Such a system would document and analyze participatory efforts in a way that served to guide practice, policy, and funding.

The first step toward the development of such a system would be to clarify what needs to be researched and developed. At national, state, and local levels, information about program needs can be gathered within the various segments of the field through conferences, interviews, and questionnaires. Individual programs can use meetings of learners and staff to determine whether there are special questions that the programs should be investigating for their own purposes. It is crucial for learners to play a major role in defining the research and development agenda.

A research and development effort must be based on an understanding of the considerable participatory theory and practice that already exists. Unfortunately, while some theoretical work is available in academic forms, there is little documentation of how learner-centered principles have been put into practice. Existing theory and practice should be identified in the various segments of the literacy and research communities where they have been developed and then documented in accessible forms.

As existing and new findings are documented, the resulting information must be made available through a training, networking, and publications system that gets useful information into the hands of practitioners, policy makers, and learners. One or more clearinghouses might be established to focus on particular geographic areas, topics, or segments of the field. These clearinghouses could publish and distribute documents to interested parties.

**Recommendation 5: Institute a Training and Networking System**

Training activities can develop the theoretical understanding and technical skills of interested parties. They can strengthen the sense of solidarity among supporters of learner-centered education. They can serve to expand the number of supporters and thereby create a political constituency. And they can provide researchers with opportunities to gather information on needs and resources in the field for further use in research and development, training and networking activities, and publications.

This training and networking system could consist of the following formal and informal exchanges, many of which could be led by learners:

- Ongoing formal and informal training opportunities for staff, learners, and others within individual programs, which could take the forms of support groups for students and staff members in which technical and other questions were discussed and which could serve as key resources for others interested in learning about participatory practice in real program contexts
- Student and staff exchanges among programs that would have clear objectives and not consist merely of unfocused visits
- Longer-term residencies or internships for practitioners in model programs
- Teacher-in-residence programs, in which an experienced teacher worked for a period with another program
- Conferences and symposia
- Targeted training and development, especially for new programs, that included not only training sessions but ongoing supervision and consultation by master practitioners and students
- Training institutes (perhaps on a regional basis) conducted by network members, for several days at a time, with ongoing exchange and support among members
- Longer-term training for practitioners (including learners who had graduated from GED programs) at the community college and university levels

- Referral services (perhaps carried out by the research and development clearinghouse system with the aid of a computerized information system) that enabled callers to locate resource people in their geographic area or with expertise in a certain technical area
- Concise, widely distributed newsletters and other practically oriented field guides prepared by practitioners and learners dealing with a wide range of instructional and management issues.

At present, too many practitioners have only a limited understanding of a few theorists and teaching techniques developed through participation in a few workshops, by reading a few books and articles, and through trial and error at the field level. Practitioners also tend to work in isolation from one another, constantly reinventing the wheel and not building on the good learner-centered work that has already been done. This training and networking system would aim at moving the field significantly beyond its present point.

### Recommendation 6: Be Prepared to Deal with Learners' and Practitioners' Personal Concerns

Learners and practitioners come to participatory programs with genuine concerns about how they will fit in. These questions are legitimate ones, stemming from previous experience in other contexts. Learner-centered activists must be prepared to work with learners and staff to respond constructively to these concerns.

*Confidentiality.* For many understandable reasons, learners can feel threatened by the idea of revealing their basic skills problems to others. However, participatory programs cannot succeed in an atmosphere of shame and fear. They must deal constructively with learners' fears of going public right up front in a sensitive and mature way. In individual counseling sessions, in support groups, and in other forums, learners must be given the chance to express their fears and decide for themselves how much they want to reveal of themselves at any one time.

*Manipulation.* Learners can be (or feel) unfairly manipulated when they get involved in new, more active roles in their programs. For example, staff or sponsoring agencies may use learners merely as window dressing at public events or give learners no more than token roles in boards of directors and other activities. Learners may also agree to participate in an activity not out of genuine interest but because they feel obliged to do so. In these cases, learners are actually involved only at the lower levels of participation shown in Figure 1 in Chapter Two.

Whether staff consciously intend this manipulation or not, learners can end up resenting the program and backing away from further opportunities for active participation. As with the issue of confidentiality, the question of manipulation must be discussed up front before activities get under way. Learners must also be given the opportunity to speak out if they feel they are being pushed into doing things they do not want to do.

Practitioners should understand the circumstances that might push them to manipulate learners. For example, they can fall unconsciously into the trap of manipulation if they rush into activities without fully discussing the purposes and implications of the activities with the learners in advance. A participatory activity can also degenerate into manipulation if the logistical resources required for smooth operation of the activity are not in place, the activity begins to fall apart, and staff members rush in to "save" the activity while effectively taking control of the activity away from the learners involved.

In the special case of hiring learners for work within the program, programs have to negotiate equitable pay rates so that learners do not feel they are not being paid a fair wage. Learners should also not be given the impression that their active participation in program activities will necessarily lead to jobs or other benefits inside or outside the program. If learners are left with that impression and the benefits do not materialize, learners are likely to feel cheated.

Learners should also have the chance to help decide who participates in which activities. Learners then need not feel that staff are choosing their favorites for such high-status roles as public spokesperson or board member.

*Leadership.* Participatory education is in many ways a question of developing leadership. Through participatory activities, students have the opportunity to learn how to become stronger leaders. But leadership does not happen just because a learner joins a participatory activity. Special technical skills (such as public speaking, running meetings, handling conflicts, and preventing ego trips), a change in thinking about oneself and one's role in the world, and an ongoing commitment are all things that many students will have to develop.

A student can learn some of these skills and traits by observing others in the program and by trial and error while participating in actual activities. Programs should also consider dealing with these leadership issues directly, through training activities for both staff and students. Such activities could include personal counseling with staff members and student-to-student discussions in support groups, classroom debates, or other student forums. Programs can also use an open-enrollment system, in which veteran students are mixed with newcomers. In such an arrangement, the veterans can serve as role models, demonstrating to the newcomers what is involved in taking active roles within the program.

Programs that have not had a history of having students in leadership roles might wonder where to start. Those who have been through this process advise that programs start slowly. Inexperienced programs need to offer a variety of participatory activities to learners and thereby provide options from which learners can choose. As activities get under way, leaders tend to emerge who in turn serve as role models for others. These experiences should be evaluated by all involved and then built upon over time. In these ways, a foundation will be established for development of student leadership.

Practitioners will also have to develop their own leadership capacities as individuals and as a force within the field.

*Moral Support.* Both learners and practitioners embarking on building participatory alternatives will face challenges to their personal security. Learners can feel embarrassed and intimidated by the prospect of taking on new roles. Practitioners may be branded as mavericks in the field and end up feeling isolated from others who stay with the herd.

These risk takers will need more than an occasional pat on the back. For example, when learners emerge from an attempt to lead a group or speak to an audience, they can feel quite uncertain about how they did. When no one steps forward to reassure them or give them feedback on their performance, the learners can feel abandoned and reluctant to take the risk again.

For these reasons, well-structured counseling, support groups, self-help projects, and other mechanisms are needed to provide the sense of community and the technical guidance that learners need. Practitioners need similar structures to help them deal not only with the special demands associated with unfamiliar new learner-centered activities but with the normal stresses of any educational program setting. Staff members' salaries and benefits also need to be adequate to support their work in the program.

One added benefit of establishing student support groups: Some one-to-one programs have reported that establishing student support groups helped them make the transition to the small-group instructional format.

*Commitment.* A high level of commitment is required if a participatory literacy effort is to succeed. How committed we are determines how much we trust each other, how willing we are to work collaboratively, how many resources we can attract to our programs, and how strong our efforts will be.

We need to commit ourselves to the process not only in principle and spirit, but we also have to set aside the time and other resources needed for these activities to succeed. The illiteracy problem is not likely to go away soon. Even the best efforts to provide quality, equitable education to all children will continue to be weighed down by poverty, drugs, and violence. Immigration will continue to increase the pool of adults with limited basic skills. And new technologies will continue to raise the levels of literacy skills expected of citizens. At the same time, demands for literacy services are growing at a rate faster than existing, overburdened programs can meet. The need for the kinds of effective literacy practices that participatory practices represent will thus remain with us for some time.

For all these reasons, active learner participation should be seen not as a fad that programs and support organizations jump onto this year and then abandon for another gimmick next year. It is a principle that should permeate the work of committed activists on an ongoing, constant basis.

## Conclusion

The preceding recommendations represent a tall order for those who want to build the participatory approach as a significant force in the literacy field. We are asked to pull together, study existing theory and practice, beware of contextual constraints, find resources to work with, establish research and development and training and networking systems, and attend to the personal needs of learners and practitioners.

Fortunately, we are not starting from scratch. Learners and practitioners have already done a good amount of work, and there are clear signs of growing interest.

We invite others to join us in creating a political constituency for learner-centered education. We will persevere because we have seen what a more efficient, human, and democratic form of education can accomplish for us all.

## Reference

Jurmo, P. J. "Learner Participation Practices in Adult Literacy Efforts in the United States." Unpublished Ed.D. dissertation, University of Massachusetts, Amherst, 1987.

*Paul Jurmo is senior program associate at the Business Council for Effective Literacy in New York City.*

# Index